understanding their world
sharing good news

Robin Thomson

Engaging with Hindus
© Robin Thomson/The Good Book Company, 2014

Published by:
The Good Book Company

Tel (UK): 0333 123 0880
Tel (US): 866 244 2165

Email (UK): info@thegoodbook.co.uk
Email (US): info@thegoodbook.com

Websites:
UK: www.thegoodbook.co.uk
North America: www.thegoodbook.com
Australia: www.thegoodbook.com.au
New Zealand: www.thegoodbook.co.nz

We are grateful for permission to use material from:
Chapatis for Tea by Ram Gidoomal and Margaret Wardell, Highland, 1994, on pages 22-24 32-33; 57-58 and *A Way of life: Introducing Hinduism* by Ram Gidoomal and Robin Thomson, Hodder, 1997, on pages 12, 16 and 42

ISBN: 9781909919105
Design by André Parker
Printed in the UK

Also in this series:
- Engaging with Atheists
- Engaging with Muslims

Contents

Acknowledgements

This book is based on what I have learned from many others—both Hindu and Christian—too many to mention here.

In preparing this I am grateful for support and constructive feedback from Hindu and Christian friends:
Raju Abraham, Ram Gidoomal, Prabhu Guptara,
Matthew Irvine, Deepak Mahtani, Sunil Raheja,
Manoj Raithatha, Kumar Rajagopalan, Charmaine Rasiah,
Basil Scott, Jagdish Sharma, Satish Sharma,
Suneel Shivdasani.

Engaging with...

Preface

Christians have a wonderful message to tell the world. As the angel said at the birth of Jesus, it is "good news that will cause great joy, *for all the people*" (Luke 2 v 10). But at times we have been slow to take that message of forgiveness and new life to others.

Sometimes it's because we have become *distracted*. There are so many things that can push the need to tell others from its central place in our calling as individuals and churches. We get wrapped up in our own church issues, problems and politics. Or we get sidetracked by the very real needs of our broken and hurting world, and expend our energies on dealing with the symptoms rather than the cause.

Sometimes it's because we have lacked *conviction*. We look at people who seem relatively happy or settled in their own beliefs, and don't think Jesus is for them. Or perhaps we have simply forgotten just how good the good news is, and how serious the consequences are for those who enter eternity unforgiven.

But sometimes it has been *fear* that has held us back from sharing the good news about Jesus. When we meet people whose culture, background or beliefs are so different from ours, we can draw back from speaking about our own faith because we are afraid of saying the wrong thing, unintentionally offending them, or getting into an unhelpful argument that leads nowhere.

This little series of books is designed to help with this last issue. We want to encourage Christian believers and whole churches to focus on our primary task of sharing the good news with the whole world. Each title aims to equip you with the understanding you need, so that you can build meaningful friendships with others from different backgrounds, and share the good news in a relevant and clear way.

It is our prayer that this book will help you do that with a Hindu neighbour, friend or work colleague and that the result would be "great joy" as they understand that Jesus is good news for them.

Tim Thornborough
Series Editor

Understanding
Hindus

Chapter one
A global faith

Hindus are the world's third largest religious community, with increasing influence on every aspect of life. Politicians, film stars and royalty consult their astrologers or their gurus. People often talk about *karma*.

Management consultants (the new gurus) tell chief executives to unlock the potential of "the Self" within, while some recommend Transcendental Meditation to relieve stress and clear the mind.

Yoga is everywhere. Doctors have begun using it to help people with asthma, arthritis or high blood pressure. Health authorities are looking seriously at the ancient Ayurvedic health system of India to see what insights might be helpful to our modern lifestyle.

Recent surveys show that increasing numbers in the West believe in reincarnation.

The New Age movement is a rainbow of beliefs and practices, but its philosophical foundations are essentially Hindu, along with ideas from Buddhism and other Eastern religions. It incorporates Hindu spiritual disciplines like meditation, yoga, and channelling occult powers.

The Hindus you meet could be doctors, pharmacists, IT professionals, business people, shopkeepers, call-centre workers, media people, your neighbours, colleagues or friends. You may have seen devotees of Krishna dancing and singing in the streets.

On the big screen, you might have seen Hindus or the influence of Hindu ideas in *Life of Pi*, *Slumdog Millionaire*, *Eat Pray Love* or *The Best Exotic Marigold Hotel*.

According to C. S. Lewis, the Hindu worldview is the major alternative to the biblical worldview.

But what is Hinduism?

You may have met Hindus or know them as friends, but still find it difficult to explain what Hinduism is.

That's because Hinduism is so diverse. One scholar described it as "probably the most varied and flexible religious system in the world". There is no founder. There is no figure like Buddha, Jesus, Confucius or Mohammed. There are libraries of scriptures and at least six major schools of philosophy.

Hindus hold widely different beliefs and follow widely different practices of spirituality and worship. Each Hindu you meet believes that their way is right—and the other is not wrong. You may feel you are grasping water, as you try to bring these ideas together. "But what do you expect?" your Hindu friend replies. "How can you grasp God? All you can say is 'Not this, not that'. Our quest for God takes us to the heights and depths of human spirituality. We have autonomy in belief. I will be glad to borrow your insights and way, and incorporate them into my own."

Hinduism contains many strands, developed over long periods of time and in different regions. The word "Hindu" was originally a geographical term, used by the Persians to describe the people of the Indus River region. Later Muslim invaders called the region Hindustan, the country of the people of Hind or Sind. In the 18th and 19th centuries the term "Hinduism" was coined to describe the religions, customs, culture and way of life of the peoples of India.

Scholars debate whether the word "Hinduism" has any meaning at all. Is it an artificial term, constructed by Europeans? Or is there an underlying unity? Some Hindus call it "the world's oldest religion", tracing it back thousands of years, or refer to the *"Sanatana Dharma"*, which could be translated "the eternal religion".

Listen to this conversation:

I arrived in Mr. Patel's home and we chatted in Gujarati for a while. I enquired about which satsang [religious gathering] he attended, his family and background. He spoke of his belief in his guru and their weekly meeting. Finally we switched to English for the benefit of my English friend. He asked what Mr. Patel believed and he responded "I am a Hindu."

I was surprised. In four years of learning Gujarati, building friendships within the various Gujarati communities, visiting temples, I had never heard anyone refer to themselves as a Hindu. And yet, when confronted with a Westerner, an English person, "Hindu" became a useful label.

from 30 Days' Prayer for Hindus

As this conversation illustrates, "Hinduism" has become a useful label for its adherents when facing the other world religions like Islam and Christianity, but many do not think of themselves as "Hindu". For them, their community is important, worship of their gods is important, and living a good life is important.

"What makes Hinduism so different from other religions is that there is no agreed list of do's and don'ts," a Hindu woman in Delhi told me once. "You are free to do what you want, as long as you don't condemn others."

Hindus use "Hinduism" as shorthand for the collection of beliefs, customs, rituals, religious practices and social relationships that have grown up over centuries. Some believe it was revealed all at once to the ancient sages. Others describe it as:

> "... more like a tree that has grown gradually than like a building that has been erected at some point of time. It contains within it ... the influence of many cultures."
>
> **K M Sen,** *Hinduism: The World's Oldest Faith*

We will use the same shorthand, referring to Hinduism, but remembering that it describes an astonishing diversity of belief and practice, a complex "family of religions". Through it all runs a strong thread of autonomy.

A way of life
It is more helpful to think of Hinduism as "a way of life" or a civilisation that has absorbed ideas from all sides and held them together. This has largely been through

the strength of the family. From one perspective every Hindu has their own unique destiny, appointed by their *karma,* which cannot be transferred. But every Hindu is born into a family in which they grow up and absorb the conduct, ideas and outlook on life of their parents and the other family members:

"I was raised in a rigidly-structured and despotically-ruled Hindu home with well-preserved traditions, well-devoted customs, and well-formulated expectations, along with, of course, a great deal of love, understanding, and exhortation. You imbibed the family culture as it were, by being a member of the family, and you emulated the family's perspective on history, art, and religion, by repeated reminders, to enhance the family's image in the local community. Into such a wonderfully strict and kind family I was born."

Mahendra Singhal, formerly
Professor of Mathematics in Chicago

What holds this way of life together? Are there any key ideas or beliefs that we can identify?

From the unreal lead me to the real
From darkness lead me to light
From death lead me to immortality.

This ancient prayer from the *Rig Veda*, the earliest Hindu scriptures, is sung daily in many schools in India. For many Hindus it reflects the desire of their heart: to know the unknowable, for the mortal to become immortal, for the darkness of this world to become light. We should be very cautious about generalisations. But it would be true to say that through the wide variety of ways of worship, works, spiritual exercises, or discipleship under a guru runs the aim of taking the seeker from the physical realm to a higher spiritual realm.

Many Hindus see life as a journey towards God and a journey towards truth. Few would say they have reached God or even that they will reach God in this lifetime, but the hope is that through repeated lifetimes they might reach God.

Ed Viswanathan, a Hindu living in the USA, answers questions from his 14-year-old son:

"Daddy, what do you or anyone try to achieve through the practice of Hinduism?

"It is easy to say 'salvation', but that is the ultimate goal. Right now, we are trying to achieve peace and harmony in life ... The Hindu way of life aids that effort ... As I told you before, it is quite easy to follow Hinduism, because Hinduism believes that ignorance is the root of all evil and true knowledge is the answer to all problems. First, try to understand the truth, and then try to practice and realise that truth. So, most of us who adhere to Hinduism are not trying to become gurus or hermits or philosophers. We are just trying to have a stress-free, peaceful life."

from Am I a Hindu? The Hinduism Primer

As you meet Hindus and develop friendships, you will experience warmth and affection. You will also encounter the wealth of their cultural and spiritual heritage.

As you learn more about what Hindus believe and practise, you may find some ideas that are very different from what you believe. You will find others that seem remarkably close. For many Hindus their God is personal, one whom they seek and whose grace they need. When describing their religious experience, they may use language that is remarkably similar to how we describe our own faith and trust in Christ.

Jitu Patel is a successful Hindu businessman. He draws strength for his work from his faith in God:

"This faith gives you immense energy and courage from within to go ahead. Everything just falls into place. It's as if the Lord is there getting me through this maze and gives me the right energy and the right time and the right opportunity. I have immense faith in the Lord."

Chapter two

What do Hindus think of Christians and Christianity?

Hindus are attracted to Jesus. Mahatma Gandhi had the highest regard for the teaching and example of Jesus, especially the Sermon on the Mount. He loved hymns like *When I survey the wondrous cross* and *Lead kindly light*.

Hindus are also attracted to the service and sacrifice of Christians, who have pioneered many areas of social concern in India, especially health and education. Many Hindus speak appreciatively of the "missionary spirit", though not necessarily of "missionaries" and their work.

But their views about "Christianity" in general may be different. Here are some very common perceptions:

1. There are many ways to God
Hindus strongly believe that there is no single way. Like

leaves on a tree, the different religions represent different ways of understanding God, who is beyond all religions. Each region or culture has its own way to God, with its own validity.

> *Ekam sad viprah bahudha vadanti*
> Truth is one; the wise call it by many names
> *Rig Veda 1.64.66*

We have already seen that Hindu identity is hard to pin down. It excludes no religious path but accepts every form of religion and every expression of spirituality.

So Hindus are happy to accept Christian prayer, and Christian faith and teaching as a valid spirituality and path to God. But as soon as Christians emphasise "one way" or seek to persuade others to change their faith, Hindus see them as exclusive and arrogant. They may view "evangelical activity" and proselytising with great suspicion. They do not see any need to change their religion or be "converted". When you talk to your Hindu friend, you will soon hear her say: "It's all the same. We believe the same". This is how Satish Sharma, a prominent British Hindu, expresses it:

> When the rain stopped falling, the Ocean gazed out at the puddles on the shore and the puddles gazed at each other and at the Ocean ... All "faiths" which are busy converting are stuck in Puddle vision, trying to separate the Ocean into Puddles and then gathering Puddles to make a big Puddle. [They] are thus revealed as being unaware of the shared Es-

sence, i.e. water. If you are aware of the essence you see the futility of the conversion game."

Leaving your religion means leaving your own community, your own people. As one caller said on a radio phone-in show discussing this question: "Religious conversion is the greatest sin on earth … it's like changing your mother".

2. Western culture is the same as Christianity

Hindus believe you are born into your community of culture and faith (and that is where you should stay). Christians are born into their community. All Western countries are perceived as Christian, so Western culture is the same as Christianity. Whatever Asians see of Western culture in the media, they assume it reflects Christianity. They want what is good there but also want to retain their own cultural identity. One Hindu put it this way: "Christianity is fine for white people, or black people. We have our own culture and way of life and you have yours. We want to keep our culture and we don't want to follow Western ways, especially immorality and family breakdown."

This same thought was expressed more strongly by a European Hindu, Michael Danilo, now living in India:

"We would gain from a critical glance at the West. From a distance, we see a mighty, glittering edifice, impressive enough to hold anyone in awe; the achievements are dazzling, the talents plentiful. If, however, we come closer, we notice cracks on the façade ... and if, uninvited, we go to the back of the building, we meet piles of garbage and are struck by a stench emanating from the foundations."

3. Christians lack commitment

Hinduism is very demanding as a religion. They pray, fast, have daily worship, and go on pilgrimages. By contrast Christianity seems very easy—you go to church and get "forgiveness"! And because Hindus are very family centred and concerned about raising their children to be "upright" people, they will think: "How would we motivate our young people to live good lives?"

4. Christians in India are poor people who were exploited by missionaries, in the past and still in the present

The gospel in India took root primarily among people who belonged to the lower castes. Many were perceived to become Christians for economic and social gain, rather than as a genuine response to the Gospel. Knowing this history, many Hindus will feel: "That is alright for them, but it's not a valid motive for changing your religion. We would not like to join them."

5. Some Hindus have had bad experiences of racism

These negative experiences are linked in their minds to Western (= Christian) culture.

Many are content to remain within their own community. They argue: "I don't even practise my own religion. Why would I convert to another?"

But others have questions, like people of any faith. Hindus outside India all have one thing in common: they belong to more than one culture. Many are part of several, especially young people, caught between the cultures of their parents, their friends and wider society ... They are asking: "Where do I belong?"

Reflect

- Do you know any Hindus as work colleagues, neighbours, family or friends?
- Have you heard any of these views expressed by them?
- Think through each of these perceptions. Can you understand the concerns behind them?
- Can you think how you might start to address some of those concerns?

Sunil's story

Although I was born in India, I came to live in England with my parents at the age of two and a half. As a young child my only contact with Christianity was through school assemblies and singing hymns; practically none of which I recall now.

I tended to think, like most of my Asian contemporaries, that England and all English people were Christian. Hence all aspects of English culture— low moral values in the media and films, the high divorce rate, football hooligans—were a reflection of Christianity.

In contrast I had my Hindu and Indian origins. I didn't really understand what that meant, but felt proud to be part of a culture dating back many thousands of years. Going back to India every few years made me sense that something was there which the West lacked.

However, I had to admit there was a certain tension within me. I knew I wasn't English but then neither was I Indian. I felt I was stuck in some halfway situation. With such thoughts as these I started to study medicine. Within a short space of time my world seemed to fall apart. I found myself surrounded almost entirely by English people. I tried to make friends with some of them, but there seemed to be such a gulf between what I expected of friendship and what they expected.

I remember that time as a period of intense

searching. I was desperately looking for something solid in my life. I tried to copy my contemporaries and live basically to enjoy myself. This included late-night parties and extensive socialising. But it didn't fill the growing emptiness in my life. I tried being busy and getting very involved with sports. But nothing I did ever seemed enough.

I knew a few Christians but I felt they were arrogant, describing Christianity as "the only way", and that they were only interested in converting people to their religion. However, it did seem strange that young people should be so religious. I had to admit that they appeared to have higher moral standards than other English people I knew.

I found within me a hunger to seek God. Nothing else in this life appeared able to satisfy me. I didn't discuss this with Christians though, because I thought they'd try to convert me. I didn't want to be persuaded by human arguments. I decided I would seek the God who created me and the whole world.

As I was from Hinduism, that's where I started — chanting prayers and learning about inner peace. I learnt from Hinduism that drawing near to God was about inner meditation and doing good. Yet within me I knew there were all sorts of thoughts and feelings which were wrong.

I decided to look at other religions, but again, I would do this without telling anyone. I found some

Christian books on prayer and was quickly challenged by them.

They talked of prayer as being open and honest with God, telling him exactly how you felt. I'd never come across such concepts before and they made a deep impression on me. As I began to learn more about this type of prayer, I found God lifted me out of my depression. I knew that it was not me, but God's power. I started to spend several hours of the day trying to pray and reach out to God.

I spoke to some committed Christians, being careful not to appear too interested, in case they tried to convert me. One of them made a comment which made a deep impression, that becoming a Christian was a commitment you made in your heart. What was important was your inner self and where that was with respect to God.

I came to the conclusion that if this was what a Christian was, then I too would follow Jesus. I had so many questions in my mind, so much I didn't understand, but it appeared to be the only way I could go. So I prayed alone, with much fear and trembling.

*You can see Sunil talking about his experience at **www.drsunil.com** under the post **Just as I am.***

Chapter three

Our approach

How do we respond to Hindu perceptions and engage with our Hindu friends?

Four basic assumptions

1. **Our focus is on people (of any faith), rather than understanding their "ism".** So our aim in this book is not to give a *theoretical* understanding of "Hinduism" but to help you relate to Hindus as people. Of course we need to understand—as accurately as possible—what Hindus believe and practise. But the real key is growing a relationship with them. As we build relationships, we will we find out what is important to them and how their beliefs impact their daily lives. We will grow in trust and respect, and learn from them in many ways. But we will also be able to share, with humility and openness, how our beliefs and our relationship with Jesus have impacted our life. The best thing we can do is to become friends—genuine, unjudging friends—with Hindus. (See chapter six for more on this).

2. **Culture can be a key to understanding people.** As we have seen, religion and culture are closely linked

for Hindus. So we need to begin by understanding their culture in general, rather than going straight to their beliefs. We have already thought about the importance of family, which is cultural as well as religious. Even young Hindus brought up in the West will have a different attitude to family—closer and more complex—from most of their non-Asian counterparts.

What is culture?

A simple definition: *"Culture is the way we do things here".*

For most of us it's unconscious and assumed—until we meet people who do things differently. Then we ask: "Why do they do that?"

Culture has many layers. The outer layer is what you see: outward behaviour, customs, festivals, institutions. But all these outward things reflect inner values and beliefs.

For example, why are some people always late for events (what you see)? It could be because:

- they are disorganised
- they have a different concept of time/events
- they have different priorities: if they meet somebody, or have an unexpected visitor, it is more important to be with them than to be on time (inner values).

And anyway, what is "late"? The definitions will be quite different in Switzerland, America, Britain, Pakistan, Iran, Nigeria, China, Japan...

Is my church culture biblical?

A good question! Many things we do in church are not necessarily biblical. They simply reflect our culture. For example: sitting in pews, men and women together, children out; starting and finishing at a set time; using an organ, piano or guitars; keeping the church building closed most of the week; not eating together every Sunday. That doesn't make them better or worse—it just means that we need to think before assuming that people of a different culture will do the same, or that what they do is in any way inferior.

3. **Major obstacles for people in responding to the gospel are linked to social structures, theological questions and issues of spiritual power.** We need to take each of these seriously, or we may become frustrated. Our Hindu friends may find the unique claims of Jesus very hard to accept. But even more difficult might be the thought that Christians come from a different social community which they wouldn't for a moment think of joining. We also need to demonstrate Jesus' love and his power over the spiritual powers that can control our lives and ideas.

4. **The church is at the heart of God's purpose.** Being Christ's disciples includes being part of the body of Christ's followers. So we need to think carefully: can our churches welcome and include people from dif-

ferent backgrounds? Are they places in which Hindus will feel accepted and belong, contributing from their culture? This is all the more important because of the strength of family and community that we have already noted.

The basic approach

Here are four principles that are the basis of our relationships with Hindus. We will return to them in chapters six to nine.

1. Love

This is the start and finish of everything we do. Love means being friends—genuine, unjudging friends—with Hindus. This is not a strategy or a means to an end. Love is the end.

2. Listen and learn

Remember the common perceptions that Hindus have about Christians and Christianity. It's good to take time to listen to, and find out more about their views, rather than jump in with what we want to say. Many Hindus are comfortable with talking about their religion. So don't hesitate to ask questions (to learn, not to find fault).

3. Present Christ positively

Our focus is on Jesus, not Christianity or church structures and institutions, though people may be interested in your practice and church traditions. Don't push or hurry. Don't argue or criticise others' faith.

4. Pray

Only God can lead us to truth, so we need to pray, as we pray for all whom we know—not just for individuals but for their families too. Many Hindus will be happy if you offer to pray for them, and it may even be appropriate for you to pray with them too.

Manoj's story

In 2007 I was living the high life. I was a success-ful businessman, buying and selling blocks of apartments throughout the country. However, as I entered the new year, my good fortunes took a downturn. As the credit crunch set in, my property business began to wobble. But this paled into in-significance as my two-year-old son was suddenly taken severely ill with breathing difficulties.

Faced with the real prospect of losing him, my wife and I collapsed to our knees in prayer. I im-mediately thought: "I am being punished". Though I was a born-and-bred Hindu, I had never really practised my faith. At school I had learnt about the Christian faith and it had resonated with me.

But as my wife and I sat in the hospital with my son's life slipping away before us, I had a power-ful sense that God truly exists, and that he alone could help in our hour of need. All the while, a Christian couple we had only recently befriended were praying for us. I was puzzled—they were not family—but grateful.

On the fourth day the consultant came and told us that our son was gravely ill—she seemed to be preparing us for the worst. An hour later, to everyone's utter astonishment, my son suddenly sat bolt upright in bed. We had witnessed what could only be described as a miracle.

Immediately I pledged to my wife that we would visit our local church to say thank you to our friends for their prayers. Within weeks I found myself walking to the front of the hall to commit my life to Jesus Christ. I was on a journey in which my previous perceptions and beliefs were utterly challenged. I felt called to re-evaluate my life and new values and priorities began to take shape.

Reflect

The best thing we can do is to become friends—genuine, unjudging friends—with Hindus.

- Who are the Hindus that you know—neighbours, colleagues, school parents, shop workers...?
- What do you know about them? Their families? Their faith?
- A first step to engage with Hindus would be to pray for one of them whom you know. Pray for their family too.

Chapter four

Who is a Hindu?

Hinduism is a way of life. It begins with the **family**. Your value within society comes not just from individual accomplishments but from your family's reputation. So your accomplishments will bring honour to the family and community; any failure or wrongdoing will bring dishonour and shame to them.

The family is not just parents and children, but three or more generations (who previously all lived together), as well as the wider family. There may be anything from thirty to a hundred people in the "close" family, including aunties and uncles, cousins and grandparents. Even though they may be living on different continents, they are all still closely interconnected.

The extended family cares for its members from birth to the grave. Parents rear their children, oversee, and sometimes arrange, their marriages, education and professions. And then, in turn, the children care for their parents in retirement and old age. When parents die, their pictures are often kept and revered; the children look to them for their blessing, even after death.

Rituals and worship

Family is the place for worship of God and the rituals that are an integral part of Hindu existence. Most homes have a shrine containing a small metal or marble image or a picture, maybe just postcard size, of the god or gods the family worships. Some flowers will be arranged before it. The shrine may be in a small room, in an alcove, or on a shelf fixed to the wall.

Every family will have its own pattern for prayer and worship—some are very strict in observing the rituals, others quite lax. Here is one family's approach:

In the early hours of the day, the women would wake the "gods" by lighting a lamp, and singing mantras or chants. The mantras often begin with the sacred word "Om". When the family rose they all gathered round the shrine. The holy books—for them the *Bhagavad Gita* and the *Guru Granth*—were opened up with great ritual. Other Hindu families might revere different holy books.

Then the gods had to be washed and fed. This meant bathing the images in a milk solution every day and covering them with a special cloth. All the ladies of the household performed this task on a rota basis. In some homes worshippers anoint the image with ghee [clarified butter], touch it with coloured powders, hang garlands round it and offer it flowers or leaves. They burn incense in front of it and perform *arti*, the waving of lamps.

Then the ladies would take turns to have a bath before approaching the shrine again. At a certain time each day, they would have another half hour of devotions when they sat and read from the holy books.

All food prepared in the home was first offered to the household gods before being distributed to the family and guests. *Prasad*, the food offered to the idols, was cooked in a particularly clean manner and dabbed around the mouth of the images or pictures of the gods. During the day members of the family might stop at the shrine to worship, offering flowers, incense and food to the image, or spend half an hour before a meal reading from the holy books. At six o'clock they "put the image to bed" after another special devotional time.

Hindu worship is known as *puja*, making offerings to the image. Some Hindus regard the images as nothing more than a pictorial representation, a visual aid to worship. Others believe that they are much more. They consider them to be living beings with the power and qualities of the deity, which can be available to the worshipper. So they show great respect and reverence, caring for them, washing, dressing and feeding them.

Other Hindus do not believe in images at all. The Arya Samaj, a powerful reform movement of the 19th century, completely rejected idol worship and is still influential today.

Christians may also find this aspect of Hindu worship uncomfortable. Like Paul (Acts 17 v 16), we can feel distressed by it. We may think we should be preaching against it. It would be good to reflect on Paul's approach to the idol worshippers in Athens (see the notes on page 117). But at this stage it is important to learn how, who and why a Hindu friend worships a particular god, without passing judgement. As we grow in our understanding of their beliefs, it will open doors of fruitful discussion.

Temple worship

Every Hindu home is a temple and place of worship. But temples outside the home also play a significant role. They are the dwelling place of the images of the gods who are cared for and honoured there.

Outside India, temples have become important visible symbols and community centres, like the marble temple at Neasden in north London, UK. It was built by one of the groups of the Swaminarayan Mission, funded entirely by donations from the community. The marble was quarried in Bulgaria, carved in India by traditional craftsmen, and shipped to London, where an army of volunteers put it all together. Other large temples are being built in the same way, all round the world. There are more than 30 major temples already in the USA, many of them in prominent positions in major cities; for example, in Tampa, Florida; Malibu, California; and Flushing in Queens, NYC.

What happens at the temple? This depends very much on the family's preferences. Some visit once a day, once a week, only at festivals—or never. Outside India many visit regularly because the temples have become the centre of community life. Congregational worship is not the norm, but many come for the morning and evening *arti* ceremony. They may also sing hymns and recite prayers. Individuals may spend time in meditation or prayer for some personal need, or consult one of the priests and receive a blessing.

Festivals

Festivals punctuate the year, based on a lunar calendar. Many are occasions for the community to get together and celebrate, often with special food. Some involve fasting and private worship in the home. Different Hindus celebrate different festivals, depending on the region in India that they originate from, or on their particular sect. Many festivals are linked to stories about the gods or figures from the Hindu epics.

Diwali is probably the best known festival in the West, celebrated with lights, fireworks, special sweets, presents and feasting. For many it includes New Year and special remembrance of Lakshmi, the goddess of wealth. Shopkeepers and business people open a new set of books. One of the major stories behind the festival remembers Ram and Sita and the victory of light over darkness, good over evil.

Festivals are a good opportunity to ask your friends about the stories they represent and celebrate, and what they mean for them. Some elements are strongly religious, while others are more cultural, similar to the celebration of Christmas in the West.

The life cycle and stages of life

Family is also the place for rituals that mark the cycle of life—including birth, the child's naming day, the first haircut, the sacred thread ceremony, marriage, childbirth, and finally death.

In the classical tradition there were four stages of life for a Hindu man:

1. **The student stage of knowledge (*brahmacharya*)** —the boy was initiated through the sacred thread ceremony to become a man and study the Vedas.

2. **The married householder, building up one's fortunes (*gryhasta*)**—the most significant stage. The duty to marry, continue the family and care for it, was a social and religious requirement.

3. **Retirement from the world, beginning to secure one's spiritual welfare (*vanaprastha*)**—"going into the forest" to live as a hermit, meditating on the scriptures. In practice this more often involves handing over responsibility to the next generation and spending more time reading the holy books.

4. **Complete renunciation of the world, preparing for the ultimate detachment from life (*sannyas*)** —an optional stage, perhaps an indication that a person was near the end of the cycle of rebirths.

Caste

You are born into your family. That is part of the wider, extended family, which is part of the wider community of caste. Caste is a complex social system whose exact origins are unknown. It is both religious, with the division of four major groupings (*varna*), and occupational, with hundreds of different sub-groups (*jati*). Caste identity is also found among South Asians of other faith backgrounds.

There are strong ideas of pollution and separation—so distinctions need to be maintained, especially with regard to marriage and food habits. Most expect to marry within their own caste, or sub-caste, looking for the most "suitable" boy or girl from the same background. But these days increasing numbers are marrying without concern for caste background.

Caste is also based on the concept of mutual interdependence. Each group performs its functions for a larger whole, serving the community. For most people, their loyalty and commitment are to their own caste people.

Caste can be very controversial, as it is seen as divisive and hierarchical. India has taken many steps to abolish discrimination, and in practice distinctions have also been broken down by modern urban life. Outside India many regard caste as irrelevant. It is also true that more Hindus outside India come from "higher" castes and so there is less sense of difference.

Hindus outside India

Hindus spread through South East Asia in the early centuries of this era, mostly through trade. The British Empire resulted in many moving to work in places like Fiji, South and East Africa, and Central America. The last 65 years have seen waves of migration, partly following the partition of India and then civil war in Sri Lanka, as well as for economic reasons.

Hindus in Britain and North America are generally successful and prosperous, well integrated into the larger society, many of them professionals. In the USA Indians (mostly Hindu) are among the highest achieving communities in education and the professions.

In the UK, British Hindus, as Lord Bhikhu Parekh has

said: "quietly concentrated on building their careers, holding their families together ... and giving their children the best education they could afford".

Despite this, there can be a tendency for Hindus to feel unrecognised, because of the much higher profile of Muslims, especially since 9/11 and 7/7. There are also deep concerns among Hindus living in the West about conversion, and the perception that poor people are still "being converted" to Christianity in India (which is seen as evidence of exploitation). Young people in particular face issues of identity in multicultural, but still divided, societies. Many have faced discrimination in some form.

Diaspora Hindus are now increasingly being challenged to articulate their religious traditions in a way that places more emphasis on doctrine and how it applies to life issues.

Summary

Hinduism is a way of life, based on some common beliefs and held together by its enduring social structure. Family and community are fundamentally important. That is where you are born, raised and find your Hindu identity, more than through your personal belief.

Ramesh's story

I was brought up in an orthodox Hindu Brahmin home. When our family moved to Britain, we actively practised the faith and I did my daily prayers. When I was 15, I went to India to have the thread ceremony, which entitles male Brahmins to pursue God and seek salvation.

At the temple I discovered the reality of caste. Non-Brahmins were very deferential to me. They were far more pious than I was, yet they were not allowed to enter with me and offer prayers in the place where the idols were.

I struggled to accept a god who excluded some by virtue of their birth. I rebelled and became an atheist, with my faith in science.

At university the first Christian I met told me my grandmother was burning in hell, which made me very angry. Another Christian, Neil, became a good friend and began to share the gospel, through his friendly, helpful attitude as well as his words. I don't remember what he said, but he gently challenged my cynicism about people and situations.

As I studied chemistry and learnt about the intricacies of our world, I accepted there must be a God. Neil gave me a New Testament and I read through Luke's Gospel twice. I attended Bible studies and asked what must have seemed awkward questions. At one point I remember kneeling outside a church and saying: "God, if you are real, I want to know".

Eventually I went to a church with Neil and heard the gospel preached from Luke. I gave my life to Christ on 5th May 1985. From my background of abandoning Hinduism because of caste division, the key verse for me is Galatians 3 v 28: "There is neither Jew nor Gentile, neither slave nor free, nor is there male and female, for you are all one in Christ Jesus."

Chapter five

What do Hindus believe and practise?

There is no such thing as an "average" Hindu. Hinduism has no central organisation regulating what people believe or how they practice religion. You can be a theist or an atheist, a sceptic or an agnostic, and still call yourself a Hindu if you accept the Hindu system of culture and life. What counts is conduct and not belief.

In that case, is there any point in trying to answer the question in the chapter heading?

It would certainly be inappropriate to approach any Hindu with a fixed idea of what they are *supposed* to believe, perhaps based on what their scriptures teach. The best way to explore any particular Hindu's beliefs is to ask what that specific individual believes, what specific practices they undertake, why they do it, and what they get out of it. That will help you understand what is important to them from the range of things that Hindus believe and practise.

But there are some major beliefs, or themes, which are widely accepted across the traditions. They give us a framework for understanding, or avoiding misunderstanding. What follows may feel complicated and difficult, but it is worth thinking carefully about these ideas, and working at understanding the words in this chapter that describe a Hindu's world view. Here are the central five:

1. **God:** God is at the centre of life, manifested under countless different names, forms and images.
2. **Suffering and justice:** How do you explain the injustice and pain of life? *karma* and *sansara*.
3. **Duty and a way of life:** Fulfilling your *dharma* could be the best summary of the Hindu way of life.
4. **Family and society:** Every Hindu is born into a network of relationships.
5. **The goal of life:** There are many ways to reach salvation.

Let's work through each of these to see the range of beliefs they encompass.

1. God

God is at the centre of life for Hindus, the ultimate and absolute reality. The whole purpose of life could be summed up as coming to know God and to achieve some kind of union with God.

There is only one God, the Supreme Being. But when we ask what is meant by God, the answers are literally limitless, because God is manifested under countless different names, forms and images.

There is a spectrum of beliefs about God. At one end is the understanding of God as an impersonal principle. Some say that the best description of God in Hindu thought is "energy". "When I dance, I feel the energy of the cosmos flowing through me," says Neera Kapur, an Odissi dancer from Kenya.

For some, this eternal principle is the only reality. There is no Creator God distinct from the world. This is the Absolute One, known as *Brahman*. A Hindu might say: "We cannot describe it: we can only say about it *'neti, neti*—It's not this, it's not that'".

This view is known as monism—God as the only reality. The universe is God and God is the universe. In Sanskrit it is called *advaita* or "non-duality". In this view the Self is actually one with God, though trapped by ignorance. It needs to realise its true nature to be liberated. There are different forms of this approach held by revered teachers and scholars of the past.

This view of God is at the more abstract, philosophical end of the spectrum. It has been widely spread in the Western world through popular writers like Aldous Huxley and the scholar Dr. S. Radhakrishnan, Professor of Philosophy at Oxford, both writing in the 1930s. Many New Agers follow this kind of understanding. A sense of this has also been picked up in popular culture in films like *Star Wars* and *Avatar*.

A more personal Supreme God?

Advaita monism is deeply influential. But the great majority of Hindus believe in God as in some sense personal, receiving worship and devotion. The two most important deities are Vishnu and Siva. Their followers worship them as supreme. Some worship the Mother Goddess (Devi), under different names, as supreme. In that sense we could call them monotheist.

But the supreme gods are accompanied by many, many other gods and goddesses, because God is manifested under countless names, forms and images. No single idea of God can do justice to the reality. One Hindu I spoke with said:

> "We believe in One Supreme Being, but we choose the form (or formless way) that we worship. I value that freedom, and I believe that is the main difference between us and Christians."

"One God, many manifestations" could be considered a cardinal belief of Hindus.

The gods who manifest God vary greatly. Some, like Lakshmi (goddess of wealth) and Parvati, are the consorts of the two major gods. Others can be thought of as forces of nature, like Agni the god of fire, Indra, god of the storm, or Surya, the sun. Two very popular gods are Ganesh, the elephant-headed son of Shiva and Parvati, and Hanuman, the monkey god. Ganesh is especially popular as he removes obstacles and brings good fortune. Many pray to Ganesh at the start of a journey or any new enterprise.

Hindu stories speak of Vishnu as having descended to the earth ten different times as an *avatar* or incarnation, to destroy evil and protect the good.

Rama

Krishna

Ganesh

Hanuman

Illustrations: Wikimedia Commons

"Whenever righteousness declines and unrighteousness arises, then I manifest myself upon the earth. For the deliverance of the good, for the destruction of evildoers and for the re-establishment of righteousness, I am born from age to age."

The Bhagavad Gita 4.7-8

The most popular incarnations are Rama and Krishna, who are widely worshipped.

Village Hindus in India also worship local gods, who are seen as guardians of that place. They are sometimes described as the representative of the major gods. When praying for protection and prosperity, people may also be very conscious of demons and spirits, who need to be placated.

Hindus are free to choose the gods or goddesses on whom they focus their devotion and prayer—their *ishta devata*—often chosen by family tradition. They give primary worship to one or a few gods, while acknowledging the existence of the others.

Most Hindus worship their gods in the form of images. As we saw in the previous chapter, Hindus vary greatly in their views of images. Here is one devotee's experience:

From 8 years old I believed in God. We followed our guru as well as the gods of our village. We used to go around with flags, offering incense and bowing down to the images or sacred places. We believed there was only one God, but many ways to him. I tried my best to serve God and the images. They told me to do various things; for example, on Thursday no eating meat or drinking; on Sunday no cutting your nails; on Tuesday no washing clothes late at night. I tried to do my best as I was scared of them. They told me that I would find God by my works, but I always let myself down.

At the other end of the spectrum, some Hindus are agnostic or atheist but still Hindu—part of the social and community structure, and often proud of its achievements.

2. Suffering and justice

How do you explain the injustice and pain of life? Why is the world so unfair? All human beings, in every religious or non-religious tradition, have wrestled with these questions. In the Bible, Psalm 73 and the book of Job are two of several passages questioning God about how unfair and unjust life appears to be.

The Hindu answer to this problem is the law of *karma*—cause and effect in the moral realm. Whatever you do, good or bad, you will reap the consequences. "What you sow, you will reap" is a principle that is found in many other traditions—including Christianity (see Galatians 6 v 7).

This works up to a point, but there are so many exceptions. The corrupt traders or ruthless dictators who prosper, and the innocent people who suffer every day—how are they reaping what they are sowing? In the Bible, the ultimate answer is that there is a judgment to be faced at the end of one life. But for Hindus the principle of *karma* is extended to many thousands of lives, past and future.

Your situation in this life is based on your behaviour in past lives. And the way you behave now determines your status in the next life. All human and animal life is caught up in the cycle of birth and re-birth—reincarnation. This is known as *sansara* ('the wheel').

3. Duty and a way of life

For the ordinary Hindu, the most important thing is to fulfil your duty—to the gods, your guru and your family, according to your unique place in the social structure. This duty is called *dharma*, a word which can also be translated "religion", a principle behind the universe.

Dr Jagadish Sharma, a retired educationist explains:

Dharma refers to the nature of things or people. For example, the sun gives warmth and light as its dharma. While a guru's dharma is to teach good things, a child's dharma is to learn. Dharma means the right way of doing things ... The world is real, it is governed by the laws of nature ... That is dharma ... much more than religion; it is a complete guide for good living.

The great stories of the Hindu epics are about people who fulfilled their *dharma*. Fulfilling your *dharma* could be the best summary of the Hindu way of life.

4. Family and society

Every Hindu is born into a network of relationships. We have already emphasised family and community as the bedrock of Hindu society (see chapter four). It is this social structure which has held together the diverse beliefs and practices of Hinduism.

And this is not just a matter of chance or choice. Each

person's birth into their family, and their duty in life (*dharma*), are uniquely appointed by the law of *karma*. Whatever they believe, they must seek to honour and uphold the values of their family and community. This is their *dharma*, and this ensures that they accumulate good *karma*. My friend Ramesh illustrates these principles:

> My parents loved to remind us of the story of Ganesh, the son of Shiva and Parvati. His parents offered great rewards if he or his brother could circle the world first. His brother ran off to attempt it, but Ganesh just walked round his parents: "you are my world," he said. The lesson was clear: parents embody God and are worthy of great respect.

5. The goal of life

There are different goals according to our stage of life and our place in society. But the ultimate goal is liberation or release from the succession of lives, known as *moksha*. In each of us there is the essential Self, the innermost essence, the *atman*—the same in all living creatures (see *Bhagavad Gita 5.18*). For all practical purposes we could call this the "soul", though it is not exactly the same in all traditions.

When the Self is completely pure, it leaves the cycle of birth and rebirth and goes back to being part of *Brahman*. Some believe this means absorption into Brahman. One Hindu described it like becoming "a wave in this big ocean, sort of merged in this cosmic world ... I am just a small particle. And yet I am like a microcosm in this macrocosm. I feel unified with this."

Other traditions believe in a distinction and awareness of one's own identity; the soul continues to serve and worship God, who remains separate and supreme above all.

Some believe there are interim places of bliss or punishment. People speak of loved ones going to their "heavenly abode" and say that they will meet again.

For many Hindus the hope of *moksha* is quite distant, and the search for peace (*shanti*) and protection in this life is much more immediate.

Some find peace in this whole process. If it is all controlled by *karma*, why strive for what was never intended for you in this particular life? Many do struggle—to overcome, to improve, to find resolution.

Paths to salvation

In Hindu thought, there are many ways to reach salvation, such as meditation, devotion and worship, fulfilling duty, doing good deeds or performing rituals.

The three major ways are often listed as:

- **The way of knowledge**—*jnana marg*
- **The way of devotion**—*bhakti marg*
- **The way of action**—*karma marg*

These are worked out in different combinations in daily life. All are equally valid, but the most important, undoubtedly, is the way of devotion (*bhakti*), whether through offerings, singing *bhajans* (songs of worship and devotion), dancing or simply contemplation of the deity. The worshippers at the shrine seek *darshan*—literally "sight" or "viewing", but with the sense of an audience with the monarch.

Krishna states that all the ways are summed up in worship and devotion to him:

> "He who offers me with devotion a leaf, a flower, fruit or water, that devout offering of a pure minded one I accept". *The Bhagavad Gita 9.26*

Sacrifices and rituals are another way to obtain power, including recitation of a mantra, which is a spell, a sound that has power. The word *"OM"* is the ultimate mantra, the most important sound, expressing the power that created the universe.

Why are gurus so important?

There is no single path for Hindus. The ideas and beliefs we have looked at here are only a small part of a limitless range. Many celebrate this diversity; others find it bewildering. They need somebody to provide a clear and simple way. This is why the guru is such a vital part of Hindu life.

Guru is usually translated "teacher" but could also be "way". The guru is a person who has *experienced* God, and so can speak with authority and come from any caste or social background. Some have a small group of disciples; others inspire millions to follow them, in India and around the world.

Gurus have been going to the West for the last hundred years or more, but became especially popular from the 1960s. Within India, the best known for many years was Satya Sai Baba, who was believed to have miraculous powers and had over 50 million followers. He died in 2011. Sri Sri Ravi Shankar in Bangalore is one of the most influential today, with his "Art of Living" movement. You will often see pictures of these gurus hanging on the walls of Hindu homes.

Some gurus have appeared more interested in gaining power and money. Bhagwan Osho Rajneesh had 93 Rolls-Royces at the height of his power. Others sincerely want to teach the truth that they have discovered.

A key to their appeal is the framework they have developed for summarising Hinduism in simple and memorable ways. They have created a "package" that ordinary people can follow, perhaps after years of trying to work it out for themselves. They also bring a direct, powerful experience of God.

Rajneesh told his followers to "kill the mind", to give up their attempts to find God or truth through thinking. They should just follow his practice and do what he told them. Other gurus give a mantra, or a simple formula or routine of rituals or mind exercises. For example, Sri Sri Ravi Shankar says:

"Become God to each other. Do not look for God somewhere in the sky, but see God in every pair of eyes, in the mountains, in water, in trees and in animals.

Morari Bapu, another well-known guru, sums it all up in three values:

"Truth, love, compassion."

The followers must accept the authority of their spiritual master and carry out their teaching and practice. Many consult their guru before making a journey or starting a new business venture. Elizabeth Gilbert popularised Hindu ideas with her best-selling book *Eat, Pray, Love*. Here is how she describes her devotion to her guru:

> I started meditating every morning on the ancient Sanskrit mantra the Guru gives to all her students (the regal *Om Namah Shivaya*, meaning "I honor the deity that resides within me"). Then I listened to the Guru speak for the first time in person, and her words gave me chill bumps over my whole body.

Is yoga part of Hindu spirituality?

Yoga has become so popular around the world that it has become controversial. Is it a religious activity? Does it belong to Hinduism? Can people of other faiths use the exercises without accepting the teaching?

The word *yoga* is used in different ways. It literally means "union", from the same root as the word "yoke" in English. It can be used to describe any kind of spiritual activity. But in the strict sense it refers to a mental discipline through which the Self can attain union with the Absolute.

These mental disciplines began to be developed in India hundreds of years before the Christian era. They were organised into the classical system by Patanjali (c. AD 100). He identified various types or stages, including physical exercise and breathing (sometimes called *hatha yoga*). It is these exercises that have become popular all around the world, and for which health benefits are claimed.

Today many de-link the exercises from the classical mental and physical discipline that leads ultimately to a state of pure consciousness united with the Absolute. Patanjali defined yoga as *citta-vritti-nirodha*, "the suppression of the modifications of the mind", through a series of disciplines, first to remove moral distractions and then physical distractions, through correct posture (*asana*) and controlled breathing (*pranayama*). In this sense the aim of yoga is to empty yourself, to close down all the openings and activities of the body until they cease to distract.

Has yoga today gone beyond this traditional understanding to a simple exercise plan? The debate continues.

The Hindu scriptures

Jews and Christians, Muslims and Sikhs could all be called "people of the book". Hindus have not just a book but a library—in fact a library of libraries.

The Hindu scriptures are vast and varied. Here are just some of the main ones. (All dates are approximate. Some scholars give much earlier dates).

The Vedas (written 1500 – 1000 BC)

These are the most authoritative scriptures, known as *sruti* ("heard"). They are considered to be eternal, and their contents to be heard directly from God.

They are a vast collection of hymns, stories, rituals, magic and philosophy. The earliest collection is the Rig Veda ("Songs of Praise"), over 1000 sacrificial hymns to gods of sky and earth, and the elements of nature. Sacrifice was fundamental to the Vedic religion. We see the increasing power of ritual and the priests in the later hymns of the Rig Veda and the three other collections, the Yajur Veda, Sama Veda and Atharva Veda.

These are known as "The Four Vedas", and for some these *are* the Vedas. But the Vedas include other texts, especially the next major collection...

The Upanishads (written 700-200 BC)

These are philosophical and mystical dialogues, also known as the *Vedanta*, the "end of the Vedas". They moved behind the gods and rituals to search for the one underlying reality—the Self, or innermost essence of a person (*atman*), identical with the innermost essence or One behind all reality (*Brahman*).

Atman = Brahman. This is the central insight of the Upanishads, summed up in the phrase: "*Tat tvam Asi*", "You are That". This idea leads to the other great innovation introduced in the Upanishads—belief in reincarnation and the law of *karma*.

The Upanishads are the foundation of Hindu thought. One scholar described the shift like this:

> The gods recede into the background, the priests are subordinated, sacrifices are looked down upon, contemplation takes the place of worship and the acquisition of divine knowledge takes precedence over the performance of rites and ceremonies.

The Epics (written 300 BC – 300 AD)

Other scriptures are in the category called *smriti* ("remembered")—these are texts of popular belief and practice. The most popular are the two great epics that have been recited, sung and acted out over many generations, with tremendous impact. They represent popular religion, with spiritual and practical lessons from the behaviour of gods and human beings.

- **Mahabharata**: the longest poem in the world—the story of the Pandava and Kaurava families, the conflict of good and evil, and much, much more.
- **Ramayana**: the story of Rama—an example of obedience and *dharma*, even through suffering.

The Bhagavad Gita (written 500 BC – 200 AD)

The *Bhagavad Gita* (The Song of the Lord, The Divine Song), though brief, is probably the most influential of all Hindu scriptures. It is part of Mahabharata, and was added at some point.

The story tells of Arjuna, the Pandava leader, who faces the dilemma of having to kill his relatives in battle. Krishna, his charioteer, instructs him. This lesson in *dharma* brings together the different strands of Hindu belief and practice in a masterly synthesis:

- God is the One behind the universe, but can be related to in the person of Krishna.
- All paths to salvation are good. But the best is to focus *bhakti* (devotion) on Krishna.
- Action without desire is a key ethical principle, along with the traditional social order and stages of life.

Sheela's story

I was born in India but when I was eighteen, I went to Kenya to be married. In 1966 the whole family left Kenya and came to Britain. We found it very difficult coming to a strange country and adjusting to the different lifestyle.

I was a practising Hindu but was finding that Hinduism did not satisfy me. I started searching for an answer to my difficulties. One day I shouted out to God: "Please come and help me".

Shortly afterwards, a friend suggested I try the Radha Soamis (a popular spiritual path led by Gurinder Singh Dhillon). My whole family went to their headquarters at Beas in the Indian Punjab. I took an oath not to eat meat or eggs. The Master gave me a mantra on which to meditate. I repeated it daily for two and a half hours but still didn't have peace and security. Then I began to think: "I became a Radha Soami to receive peace. If I haven't got it, I have been cheated." I asked God: "I do all the correct things. Why haven't I got peace?"

I went to visit my son, who told me he had become a Christian and invited me to church. I said, "No". But he left a Bible on the table in the sitting room. I started to read it and at once it interested me. After two weeks I wanted to go to church. I found it very different from what I had imagined. The people were so caring and friendly.

When I returned home, I started to read the Bible

regularly. Very, very slowly I began to understand. I had no sudden dramatic experience. Two years later I was baptised. I was afraid to tell my in-laws what I had done. But my behaviour changed and they saw I was different. Eventually I told them why. At first they totally ignored me. Then they got very angry. But finally when they saw I was happy, they accepted what I had done.

I now have peace and security. I pray and get so many answers. I don't ask for money and things like that. I pray that God will use me.

Reflection

Hindu beliefs can be very diverse. Ask your friend the questions at the beginning of the chapter:

- Which path (or paths) do they follow?
- Which gods do they particularly worship and do they follow any gurus?
- What is their practice of prayer and other spiritual activities?
- How do they understand *dharma*?
- What is the goal of life for them?
- What scriptures do they read, listen to, watch?
- When and how often?

Concentrate on what it means for your friend and listen with respect and attention.

- Get hold of a copy of the *Bhagavad Gita* and read it (it's very short).

Engaging with Hindus

Chapter six

Love

Remember the four actions listed in chapter three? They are the basis of our engagement as Christians with Hindus.

Being friends

Love is the start and finish of everything we do. Love means being friends—genuine, unjudging friends—with Hindus. This is not a strategy or a means to an end. Love is the end.

That sounds very simple, and in one way it is. Depending on the context, it could include taking time to stop and talk with neighbours or a local shopkeeper, having a drink with work colleagues, visiting people at home, doing things together, inviting people to your home, and so on. If you are genuinely interested in someone, conversations should flow naturally.

Visiting and supporting people in times of crisis—for

example, ill health or bereavement—is another mark of friendship and is deeply appreciated.

When Tamils arrived in London, escaping the conflict in Sri Lanka, many of them faced severe difficulties in adjusting to financial and social pressures, recovering from the trauma of war, and understanding their children as they grew up in a different culture. Churches were able to reach out in loving service.

It is very important that we avoid "using a difficult situation to preach" instead of genuinely supporting people. One Christian from a Hindu family said: "When I tried to share something with my mother in a time of difficulty, she said: 'This is what Christians are like; they pounce on you in your difficulties!'"

Hospitality is a huge part of Asian culture, so don't hesitate to accept an invitation to visit. When you visit a Hindu home, you will be warmly received and always offered something to eat or drink. Remember that, when somebody comes to visit you. Don't say: "Would you like something to drink?" as you may get a polite refusal. Ask: "What will you have—tea, coffee, cold drink...?" and make sure you serve something, even if only a glass of water is accepted. If someone says no the first time, ask again and maybe again (that's Asian hospitality).

Inviting people to your home will certainly be appreciated, although some may be anxious about what you might serve them, especially if they have strict dietary requirements, which your kitchen might not adhere to. The vast majority of Hindus are vegetarian, and for some this excludes anything made with eggs, like cake or biscuits. While you wouldn't serve them meat, some might be worried that you cook it for yourselves. Occasionally this might mean that they agree to come and then don't turn up. The best way to avoid misunderstanding may be to invite people for a drink or snacks, rather than a meal. Tea, coffee and cold drinks are fine. When you invite people, ask if they have any restrictions. They are usually quite happy to tell you.

Here is the experience of one woman who reached out in friendship:

> I called on a lady I had met in our street. She invited me in, gave me tea and some delicious snacks. I asked her to come to our house, with her family, but she seemed a little shy. Some time later I made some scones and took them to her. The next day she brought us samosas, and we have gone on exchanging food since then.

Being friends is an attitude. So more important than what you serve is your openness and warmth, your genuine interest in the other person. The reserve that some cultures show—notably in some parts of England!—may appear like a lack of friendliness. Hospitality—especially to strangers—is not just an Asian cultural value but a biblical principle (see Matthew 25 v 35; Romans 12 v 13; 1 Peter 4 v 9; Hebrews 13 v 2).

Justice

Being friends includes concern for issues like justice. Hindus might be experiencing discrimination or feel marginalised. Your sensitivity and appropriate involvement could be greatly appreciated.

Churches have sometimes shown attitudes of racial and religious prejudice. Black Christians from the Caribbean found coldness instead of a warm welcome when they came to Britain. East African Christians never thought that Asians could follow Christ and so they did not share their faith with them for many years.

And Christian leaders have not always spoken out when society turns against immigrants, whether vulnerable refugees or well established citizens. Sometimes these attitudes arise from fear, as Christians see the growth of temples or the popularity of Eastern meditation. Instead of loving and welcoming people of other faiths, Christians have been tempted to avoid them.

Genuine love could mean speaking out and acting for justice. Sometimes it is just a matter of taking the initiative to cross barriers.

A young woman in East London described her attempt:

When the mothers come for their children after school, they stand in two groups. The Asian mothers are on one side and the white mothers on the opposite. They don't talk to each other. They don't even make eye contact. Last Tuesday I went and stood next to the Asian mothers.

Working together with Hindus

One of the best ways to get to know people is to do things together.

This could be as an individual or with the whole family. From talking about sport you might progress to spending time together watching or playing something. You might exchange DVDs: if you haven't seen any Bollywood films, they are very entertaining! Your children might play together, or you could take them to the park. It could be something practical that your neighbours do for you, or you do for them.

It could be at more of a community level. Can you engage with common concerns, along with Hindu (and maybe other) communities in your area? For example:

- the need for community facilities
- drugs and gangs
- racist bullying
- language teaching and learning
- relationship advice, eg: dating, marriage
- drama, arts, dance, music and sports clubs
- care of elderly people
- ethical questions like abortion or euthanasia

You might be a school governor, on the PTA, or involved in other ways in school matters. You could make a particular effort to find out the concerns of Hindu (and other) parents, and work together with them.

I was involved in taking the Organ Donation campaign into the South Asian community. This helped me into many conversations with Hindus, starting with kidney disease, then moving on to my own story, as I had a transplant myself. We then moved to why Hindus don't give and why I would consider giving as a Christian. We became very close and had interesting discussions about our beliefs.

Deepak Mahtani

Your church may already be engaged in activities in the local community. Could you include Hindus more in them, either by inviting them to take part or by looking for things that you could do together with a local temple or other Hindu community group?

The UK's Hindu Christian Forum has been exploring a project in which local churches and temples or community groups work together in a programme called *Serving our Elderly*—one of the biggest issues of modern times, which not many groups want to deal with.

Compromise?

Some Christians might be hesitant: would that be compromising our faith? Could it be a distraction from more important tasks which are part of our mission?

In fact, finding ways of working together with Hindus is an important demonstration of our love and concern. We are serving others and contributing to the common good. We are building relationships of friendship and trust. As we do so, we begin to get behind the stereotypes. These are things that we should be doing.

Working together need not compromise our faith. It's true that some might suggest activities that would include joint worship—perfectly acceptable to most Hindus but not to Christians. If this happens, you can respond without offence; just explain that you would not be comfortable to do this.

In a Midwestern city of the USA, there was racial tension against the immigrant Indian community. A church leader suggested a community dinner with the Hindus and Sikhs. This broke down walls of suspicion. It was followed by visits and regular discussion, from ways of working together for their communities to directly personal spiritual matters. They have established a high level of trust and mutual respect.

In London a concert at a Hindu temple was advertised to the local community as part of "Inter Faith Week" and several Christians attended. "It was really good to meet Hindus there," they commented. "It helped us all feel more confident about visiting each other in future, as they had been hesitant to have links with Christians."

If all this seems fairly obvious, that's because it is! We are simply repeating the command to "love your neighbour as yourself". It isn't rocket science; it doesn't require special qualifications; anybody can do it.

But it does mean putting others before ourselves. Sometimes it will take time and effort. We may need to say "no" to other very worthwhile activities. Sacrificial love can only be sustained from the love and forgiveness of Jesus in our own lives.

The result will be relationships of trust which we can enjoy. We will be able to talk together openly about the things that matter, and share the good news that we have experienced.

Reflection

- What has been your experience of giving and receiving hospitality with Hindus? How would you take this further?
- Are you aware of particular issues that Hindu communities are facing? Have you discussed any of them with Hindu friends or community leaders? What is your response to these issues?
- What are the "common concerns" that you could engage in?
- What groups and activities (sports, book groups, music, etc) are you involved in that you might invite a Hindu friend to?

Chapter seven

Listen and learn

Remember the common perceptions that Hindus have about Christians and Christianity. It's good to take time to listen, rather than jump in with what you want to say.

As you start building relationships, you will already be asking questions and learning new things. You may have exchanged favourite dishes or compared sporting enthusiasms.

This give and take is a good way to continue your relationship. From food you can go on to learn about families and other areas of culture. As you spend time with your friends, you will find much that is common, but you will also encounter some big differences.

Some will be refreshing, like the way that children greet adults and show respect for elders. Others may be challenging; for example, different views about the use of alcohol, or the role of the sexes and the way people sit, or don't sit, together. You will have learned new names and pronunciations—and it's important to get them right, so don't hesitate to ask them to be repeated, or write them down.

From culture the step to talking about God and religion is very small, because they are closely linked. Continue to ask questions and be curious.

Asking good questions

Festivals are a good place to start, because everybody can describe what happens. They include a wide range of practices, from food (or fasting) to clothes, rituals, stories and prayers. Some are purely cultural; others have a religious basis. It isn't always easy to separate them.

As you ask questions, you will find some to be very knowledgeable, able to explain things and articulate their meaning clearly. Others will be much more vague as to the purpose or meaning, as with people of any faith background or none. You will find the level and type of topic that your friends are comfortable to talk about.

Some may talk about meditation. Some will describe physical activities—perhaps yoga, fasting or dietary requirements. Many Hindus fast on certain days, like Monday for Lord Siva. Others will talk about the importance of good deeds and moral behaviour.

I asked Chandra what his parents had taught him about Hinduism as a child and he was quite vague. But then he told me how he had enjoyed the festivals (food and fireworks) and the moral lessons they had instilled in him, mostly from the stories in the epics.

It may all fit together quite coherently, or it may still seem to you to be a rather random collection of experiences and practices that make up your friend's identity as a Hindu.

Life of Pi is a popular novel, turned into a film, that reflects Hindu culture. This is how Pi explains it:

> I am a Hindu because of sculptured cones of red kumkum powder ... because of garlands of flowers and pieces of broken coconut ... because of the fragrance of incense, because of flames of *arti* lamps circling in the darkness ... because of colourful murals telling colourful stories, because of foreheads carrying, variously signified, the same word—faith. I became loyal to these sense impressions even before I knew what they meant ... I feel at home in a Hindu temple.

Your Hindu friend may feel very similar—they are committed to being Hindu because of a whole host of experiences.

Visiting

A good way to learn more is to visit a Hindu temple. Your friends will be happy to take you (the best way to go), or you may arrange to go yourself, on your own or with others. You will find contacts on page 122 if you need help to organise a visit.

Each temple has its own style, but generally Hindus visit the temple as individuals, rather than for structured worship. So in most temples you are free to walk around, observe and ask questions. Some temples have clear directions for visitors, while others are more informal. When you arrive you will need to remove your shoes (there are clearly marked places for leaving them). Some temples have set times for *arti*, a ceremony where an offering of fire is made to the gods, usually a lamp or candles on a tray containing fruit or flowers, which is waved before the images. At these times the worshippers may gather together, men on one side, women on the other.

You are free to observe, and you will always be welcome to participate, though you don't need to. After the *arti* the lamp may be brought round and people are invited to wave the warm air towards them, receiving the blessing. Sweets may be offered to the worshippers: these are *prasad*, a gift from the gods. You are completely free not to accept either of these. Simply say: "No thank you".

As you take this time to listen and learn, you will see similarities and differences; things that fit together, and others that don't seem to.

You may also have talked about important matters of life in general, trends in society, things that concern you both or ethical questions. Don't be too eager to get on to sharing your faith with your friends; it will happen naturally in time. Here is the experience of one Christian couple:

We were introduced to Ravi through a mutual friend. He was facing some personal difficulties and he began coming to our home on Sunday afternoons with his son. We talked about the issues he was facing and that led on to our faith. We would spend two hours every week listening to him, answering questions and trying to explain things. After some months he began to join us as we went to our church.

Reflect
- How could you listen and learn more effectively? What has been your experience of this?
- Arrange to visit a temple or community centre. Write down your impressions and if possible discuss them with your Hindu friends. Don't hesitate to ask for explanations of what you have seen.
- At Diwali (or any other festival time) try to attend one of the activities. Again, write down your impressions and discuss them if you can.
- Keep noting the questions that come into your mind, so that you can ask your Hindu friends when you meet them.
- If you can read the *Bhagavad Gita*, or any other Hindu scripture, this will give you plenty to learn from and ask about.
- There are animated versions of parts of the Mahabharata in English available to view on Youtube. They will give you a basic grasp of some of the stories and ideas in the Hindu scriptures.

Chapter eight

Present Christ positively

What is our aim as we engage further with our Hindu friends? Is it to find common ground and ways of living together in our divided society? Is it to persuade them to change their religion and be converted? Here are some suggested goals:

> To seek to know the true and living God
> along with our Hindu friends
> *which includes*
> respecting their search for God
> *and*
> sharing with them our experience of God,
> *so that*
> they will also experience God's love, grace,
> peace, forgiveness and justice shown to us all
> in the Lord Jesus Christ.

This combination of *receiving* (learning about, and respecting their search for God) and *giving* (sharing what we have experienced) reflects the example of Jesus himself. He condemned false religion, pride and selfishness. But he commended the faith of outsiders like Roman soldiers and Gentile women as they were drawn to him (see Matthew 8 v 5-13; 15 v 21-28). At the same time he invited them to focus their faith still further on him, so that through him they would find their place in the "kingdom of heaven" (Matthew 8 v 11). His life, teaching, death and resurrection opened the way to eternal life, under God's perfect rule.

So our focus *must always be* on Jesus—not Christianity or the church. We do not come from a position of superiority in our culture, philosophy or religious background. Our task is humbly—and confidently—to share the treasure that we have discovered. We are like the trader who discovered the most valuable pearl in the world and sold everything to get it (Matthew 13 v 46).

And we must never think that our job is to "change their religion". Religion does not save anyone. Christianity, as a religious system, is as powerless to save us as Hinduism is. All of us, as human beings, need to seek a relationship with God. But we cannot reach him by our own efforts: they will fail. He has offered us life, forgiveness, peace and union with him, through Jesus.

This is the good news that Jesus' followers have experienced and want to share with everybody, whatever their religious background. We have not found God by our efforts. He has found us, and our job is to humbly and respectfully point others to Christ.

Building on similarities

It is not a betrayal of our faith to appreciate and affirm a Hindus' reverence for God, their desire to know God and the devotion that many show. Hindus may tell you of the importance of faith, or about God's love. Hindus believe in prayer and seek answers to prayer. They value spiritual experience and are keen to hear about others' experiences of God or their spiritual practice.

Hindus are not necessarily more spiritual or less materialistic than anybody else (contrary to stereotypes). But they appreciate spiritual disciplines and admire simplicity of life and those who renounce material things. They are attracted by sacrificial service.

We can gladly affirm these and other aspects of Hindu belief and practice. What do we have to share in response?

Explaining good news

A great way to begin explaining about our faith is to talk about Jesus, the priceless pearl!

We are his followers and disciples. So, as a starting point, it is appropriate with Hindus to refer to him as our *guru*—the teacher who shows us the truth about God. Some followers of Christ from a Hindu background refer to him as the *Sanatan Satguru*, which means the "Eternal and True/Living Teacher".

The picture of Jesus in the New Testament Gospels shows him to be the ideal man, demonstrating love and care for all, whether poor and marginalised or rich and educated. He mixed with both men and women, religious people and "sinners". He was also a healer who answered prayer and liberated people who were oppressed, physically, socially, or spiritually. He cared more for people's inner attitudes than their rituals, allowing ritually impure people to touch him and condemning false religiosity. It is a beautiful picture that resonates with many Hindus, and is attractive to them.

Jesus was not just a man: his birth was supernatural. It was foretold by prophecies hundreds of years before. He was clearly the incarnation of God, who came to reveal God and save sinners (not condemn them—see John 3 v 17). Above all, he came to die. More than one third of the Gospels tell the story of the final week of his life. His death was a demonstration of love, a victory over evil and a sacrifice that paid the debt of sin and *karma,* and removed the barrier between us and God. When he rose again, he broke the power of death and brought the hope of life.

In John's Gospel especially we see Jesus giving *darshan* ("sight") of God, receiving devotion and opening the way to union with God: "Anyone who has seen me has seen the Father" (John 14 v 9). Jesus answers the ancient Hindu prayer:

From the unreal lead me to the real
From darkness lead me to light
From death lead me to immortality

He brings the offer of eternal life, not in the distant future after many rebirths, but here and now. He really is the way, the truth and the life.

All this, and more, can be seen in the Gospels. We can encourage our friends to read for themselves the stories about Jesus, or parables that Jesus told, or to watch a DVD depiction of the life of Christ. Tell the stories about Jesus' life, death and resurrection yourself, or if it is appropriate, open up the Bible with them to read, share and discuss.

We can also share our own experience of Jesus. He is not just a great figure from the past, but alive now and present in our lives by his Spirit. We can share our experience of prayer, of the sense of God's presence, how we have received forgiveness and the ways in which our lives have been changed, as well as the ways we have failed. We can speak freely about what it looks like practically for us to follow Jesus on a daily basis, both our "devotion" (*bhakti*) to him and our "spiritual practice" of prayer and action.

This is not only in the past. We can share from our current Bible reading what we are learning about God and about ourselves, and how we are growing as a disciple of Christ.

Other important truths
A personal God who is loving and holy
Jesus' teaching makes this clear.

God is the Creator of the world
The world had a definite beginning and it is real. The world, and we ourselves, are not God. The creation account of Genesis 1 is clear and simple.

The reality of sin

This is not always an easy concept for Hindus to understand and accept. Of course, all are aware of the obvious evil around us—violence, hatred, corruption, immorality. Some regard these as the result of ignorance of our true nature. Others focus on sin as breaking rules, whether moral or ritual. The idea of sin as rebellion and disobedience to God, to whom we are personally accountable, may be new. So is the truth that our sin separates us from God and leads to judgment.

In explaining sin, it may be helpful to focus on inner attitudes. We all have hatred, selfishness or pride, and these are just as serious as the outward actions which we may avoid. Jesus' teaching is very clear in the Sermon on the Mount (Matthew 5 v 21-22, 27-28), as is his contrast between ritual and inner attitudes (Mark 7 v 20-23).

Salvation is a free gift

While the truth of sin as rebellion against God may be new, Hindus are deeply conscious of the reality of *karma* and its serious consequences. Hindus don't need to be told that you reap what you sow. But that can make it difficult to accept the idea of salvation as a free gift through the sacrifice of Christ. For some this will immediately be liberating, a wonderful offer. Others may consider it too easy. How can another person pay for my *karma*? What will prevent me from sinning again—or more practically, how will we teach our young people not to do wrong if forgiveness is so easy?

These were the same questions that the apostle Paul

faced in Romans 6, where he points out that forgiveness through Jesus' death is actually a death to the old life. From now on we want to live in a way that pleases God, because we are so grateful for his free gift.

Here is one account of how Ram Gidoomal started to understand the good news and how it related to the categories of thought he had grown up with:

> As I read Jesus' teaching and the account of his life and death, I wrestled with my *karmic* debt. How could I ever pay this debt? I knew I was spiritually bankrupt. But I came to realise that either I would have to give up and hope for a better chance to pay it off in the next life, or believe that Christ really had paid for all my sins. I realised that no other *guru* had claimed to have paid for my *karmic* debt (my sins), only Jesus. I got on my knees and prayed for Jesus to come in and take control of my life.

Suneel Shivdasani suggests these illustrations of the truth of salvation by grace that resonate with Hindu culture.

The load of karma: One Hindu friend described his *karmic* debt as like a cartload that he was dragging. His *guru* had promised to lighten the load if he followed him. He was surprised to hear that Jesus offers to take the full load.

Sari *vs.* dowry marriage: When a Hindu girl marries, it is still common for dowry to be paid. In some cases her fiancé will not insist on a dowry but instead ask her to come "just in her sari". Any gift she then brings is brought freely, out of love. In the same way, we have nothing to bring to Jesus except ourselves. His invitation is very powerful: "Come to me all you who are weary and burdened and I will give you rest" (Matthew 11 v 28).

Life after death

This life is not the end. However, we do not face a succession of lives, but the offer of life for ever in God's presence, if we accept his free gift. Otherwise there is the prospect of judgment for those who rely on their own efforts to reach God. They cannot succeed because none of us are good enough for God's perfect standard.

Finding the bridges

Look for bridges where you can. For example, sacrifice, incarnation, light and darkness. Or ask your friends what terms they use for concepts like sin, grace or forgiveness. Remember that these concepts need to be understood in their framework of the biblical story. Similarity by itself doesn't prove anything. But it is a good starting point.

Some have made careful study of the Hindu scriptures and found parallel ideas or stories which they use to show how Christ fulfils Hindu aspirations. A remarkable example is the cosmic sacrifice that underlies the universe, referred to in several of the Vedas.

These links will be very significant for those Hindus who know their scriptures. But you also need to be very well informed to make use of them.

Chapter nine

Pray

Only God can lead us to the truth, so we need to pray for ourselves, and for our friends. We are instructed in the Bible to pray:

> "... for all people—for kings and all those in authority, that we may live peaceful and quiet lives in all godliness and holiness. This is good, and pleases God our Saviour, who wants all people to be saved and to come to a knowledge of the truth."
>
> **1 Timothy 2 v 1-2**

So

- **We pray for Hindus**, as we pray for all people, that they will experience God's love, grace, peace, forgiveness and justice shown to us in Jesus Christ.
- **We pray for the Holy Spirit to open minds and hearts**, to speak to consciences.
- **We pray for ourselves**, that we will be more lov-

ing and open, and demonstrate more clearly God's love and grace to our Hindu friends, both those whom we know personally and the many more whom we have never met. We pray for the Holy Spirit to guide us in what to ask; what to say and how to say it; for specific opportunities to speak about Jesus in ways that help the hearers move towards Christ.

- **We pray not only for individuals but for their families,** that their love and support for each other will enable God's love and grace to touch each family member, and that when one of them begins to follow Jesus, this will not be seen as negative but a source of blessing to the family. Here are two stories to illustrate this:

My sister-in-law had been unwell so I phoned her. She was feeling better and immediately asked me if I read my Bible each day. Cautiously, I replied "Yes, every morning". She replied "I'm doing the same. Do you remember you gave me a Bible 30 years ago? I kept it and have just begun to read it. Can you please get me one with larger print?" I was amazed. We have been praying for all our family for many years. It's good to persevere.

When Ravi began to follow Christ, an older Christian asked him for the names of all his family members—parents, aunts and uncles, brothers and sisters, cousins. He began praying for them by name.

30 Days' Prayer for Hindus

It may be appropriate to pray *with* your Hindu friends. Hindus welcome prayer and may be happy for you to pray for them and their family in their presence, in the name of Jesus.

Reflect
- Do you have Hindu friends you can include in your regular prayer, along the lines suggested above?

Chapter ten
Preparing for discussion

There is no formula for relationships or for conversation. It's unlikely that your interaction with your Hindu friends will go through the same stages outlined above, or that you will sit down for a structured discussion in which you can explain everything in order, as you would like.

As you develop friendships, as you begin to understand your friends' Hindu identities through the conversation and activities you share, there will be times to talk together about what you believe and why.

Here are some suggestions to help you prepare. The way you work it out will depend on your relationships, circumstances, personalities and styles!

These suggestions are not just for individual use. Many Hindus begin to sense that "something is different about Jesus" through experiencing a group of Jesus' followers loving each other (and them), and worshipping Jesus to-gether, genuinely from the heart. We will return to this in chapter twelve.

1. **Ask your friend to tell you the most important parts of their faith and how they practise it.** Listen care-fully and then try to summarise back to them what you have learned. This will help you get it clear in your own mind and prevent misunderstandings.

2. **Having heard your friend, try to outline what you have in common.** This could be a great deal, or not much, depending on each person's beliefs. There will also be real differences but it's better to focus on what is common first.

3. **This may now be the occasion for you to share your own beliefs and practice.** You may already have done this. Think through how to present Jesus, from the Gospels and from your experience, relating to what your friend has explained. This is not to contradict what they have said, but to share your own spiritu-al understanding and practice. You will need to look again carefully at your Bible, checking the references given on pages 117-119. Think how your knowledge of Jesus has impacted your life, and how to tell your spiritual story briefly and in a way that is relevant and up to date.

4. **Suggest reading the Gospels or other literature, watching a DVD or going to a website.** Explain that the Bible is your authority. You may also find it help-

ful to read a Hindu scripture like the Bhagavad Gita, or one of the epics, which will give you better understanding and lead to discussion.

5. **Be ready to listen to your friend's criticisms of Christians and Christianity**, if these have not already come up (see below). If there are misunderstandings, try to explain them. Don't be defensive; be ready to acknowledge failures. And don't respond with criticism.

6. **It may be appropriate at some point to offer gentle challenges.** There is a place to ask questions about why Hindus believe what they do and express your difficulty in reconciling what they believe with the God you know from the Bible. If you are reliant on the Holy Spirit, this can be done in a way that is neither patronising nor judgmental. It could also be at a more personal level—remember how Ramesh's friend "gently challenged my cynicism", as part of their friendship (page 41). If you have shown love and been ready to listen, your relationship will allow you to do this.

   There are different levels of interacting. Talking about beliefs is helpful for some, but sharing about practices, like prayer, can be better. Talking about heart issues, such as spiritual and moral challenges, can be the most valuable, if you get there.

7. **Your preparation will involve you studying your Bible carefully and praying.**

Reflect

- Think through how to present Jesus, from the Gospels and from your experience" (point 3 above). Go back to the description of Jesus in chapter 9 and the Bible references on page 118-9. Which stories from the Gospels will you focus on?

- What other aspects of your spiritual experience are relevant, that you could share with your friend? Keep in mind what you have learned from them about their beliefs and practices, and what is important to them. Can you discuss all that with them?

Chapter eleven
Understanding Hindu questions

We have already noted the most common Hindu perceptions about Christians and Christianity in chapter two.

1. "It's all the same"

One of the first things your Hindu friend will say is: *"It's all the same: we believe the same as you. All ways lead to God."* They may go on to say that you are arrogant and exclusive.

"Your mother is the best mother in the world—for you. But you can't say she is the only mother."

This is not the time to argue! You do need to understand and respond to this important Hindu perspective. But not with argument at this point. Remember that Hindus are born into their community and they believe that you are as well. Why should they change? Why should anyone change their religion? Within their faith community they value the freedom to make their own choices and allow others to do the same.

> "... unless a man chooses for himself, the very spirit of Hinduism is destroyed. The essence of our faith consists simply in this freedom of the *ishta devata*" [your 'chosen deity']" *Swami Vivekananda*

Some Hindus have already accepted many aspects of Christian teaching and incorporated them into their own framework. They may have great reverence for Christ, as a teacher, an example, as God (but not the *only* God).

> "I was surprised to see the Gospels suggesting the same approach toward God and humanity as my Hindu faith ... I saw that [Jesus] was saying the exact same thing as the teachers of my traditions."
> *Gadadhara Pandit Dasa,*
> *Hindu Chaplain, Columbia University*

So as you begin discussion, *listen* to your friend. Instead of disagreeing at once, you can say: "It's true that many aspects are similar. I appreciate your faith. Please tell me more about what you believe, so that I can understand better."

Depending on the response, you may learn things that are indeed similar, as well as matters where you believe differently. This may be the time to talk about them. Or it may be the time for you to offer to tell them about your spiritual experience and to focus on Jesus and what the

Bible teaches about him: "I am a follower of Jesus. He is my *guru* and teacher. This is what I have learned about him from the Bible…"

This does not directly answer the original objection but helps both of you to examine and speak out what you actually believe, and it points again to Jesus. At some point you will need to engage with the argument. Either following this conversation, or later, you could say: "May I explain what Jesus said about the way to God?"

Why did Jesus say he was the only way (John 14 v 6)?

Some preliminary thoughts, as you respond to this key question:

1. **This is not a good place to start your conversations.** It can very easily be a dead-end argument. Follow the approach recommended above to avoid that. But you do need to address it at some point.

2. **Try to understand why this question is so difficult for Hindus.** It represents a different worldview. Remember the parable of the Ocean and the Puddles (page 20)? In this way of thinking, there can only be one truth, which is universal. So there should be no differences or divisions. The fact that different views of God and how we find him *do* exist is not because

they are right or wrong, superior or inferior (as Christians are perceived to say). They are just different forms—the truth itself is beyond us. So conversion from one religion (community) is not only unnecessary but wrong.

We also believe in a universal truth—that Jesus is for all. But how do we show that this is not the same as saying that one religion ("Christianity") is better than the others (and Christians are better than others)? In what way is Jesus universal?

It may be helpful to ask your friend, if they believe that all ways are essentially the same, whether they see differences in the way people believe and practise faith, and if so, how they explain them. This may lead to an acknowledgement that there are in fact differences, which will have more significance than if you just state that.

3. We need to remind ourselves, and our friends, that we are following Jesus' words, and not our own, which would certainly be arrogant.

So what did Jesus mean when he said: "I am the way and the truth and the life. No one comes to the Father except through me"?

It seems arrogant—like Western colonial arrogance? But from what we know about Jesus' character, we will want to take him seriously.

What is the truth that Jesus reveals, about God and about ourselves? All agree that our world is full of suffering and evil. Why? Is it caused by ignorance? The Bible says that it is caused by our turning away from God to our own ways. There are laws that God has given us to live by, but we do not obey them or reach the standard that we should, not just in our actions but also in our thoughts and motives.

Far from being arrogant, Jesus showed true humility as he lived in total submission to the Father—what we do *not* do. His obedience was costly, as he suffered in our place (Hebrews 4 v 15; 5 v 8; Isaiah 53 v 3-6—written hundreds of years before Jesus). So he opened the way to God. He showed that we cannot reach God by our own efforts. We can only throw ourselves, in humility, on his mercy. And God, in his mercy, has provided the way through Jesus, by his life, his teaching and above all his death. By dying as a sacrifice for our sins, Jesus has provided God's forgiveness and taken the load of our *karma* on himself (1 Peter 2 v 24; Colossians 2 v 13).

Jesus also overcame death and all the powers of evil (Colossians 2 v 15; 2 Timothy 1 v 10). People of all faiths are seeking the eternal life of heaven and freedom from suffering and evil. The Lord Jesus, who rose again, promises to give us this life here and now.

This does not make us perfect. We still fail and do wrong. But we have received forgiveness and the power to change, day by day.

When Jesus came, it was not to tell people that they were wrong and condemn them. He came to save all people by dealing with their basic problem and fulfilling their deepest longings (John 3 v 17; Acts 17 v 26-28). This was something new (Acts 17 v 30-31) and unique. No other god, or religious leader, has claimed to pay the price for our sins—though we find foreshadowings of this in many Hindu scripture stories and prayers.

From the unreal lead me to the real
From darkness lead me to light
From death lead me to immortality.

Jesus answers this prayer, as he reveals to us the truth, about God and about ourselves. If we understand the universal problem, then we may be able to understand the universal solution that Jesus provided. It is a solution to which every human needs to respond. Even those born in a devout Christian home have to choose at some point to accept this good news and submit their lives to Jesus as Lord.

I sat with a close friend, a senior government official in Delhi. We were reflecting on different religious experiences. What did we have in common? What were the differences? What about the claims of different religious leaders (his daughter followed a guru)?

"Ultimately all religions involve surrender," said my friend. "You surrender your will to God. But it does make a difference who you surrender to."

2. "Christianity is just a part of Western culture"

Another common perception among Hindus is the apparent link between Christianity and Western culture.

You can point out that you strongly agree about the failures of Western culture, and show that following Christ is different. You may have to acknowledge failures of Christians in the past or present, along with the many positive contributions. It is vital to clarify the difference between culture and following Jesus, and show that you are not concerned for them to "become Christians" but to encounter God's love through Jesus.

As mentioned earlier this is not about a change of religion or culture. In addition to the close connection between religion and culture, religious communities are legally defined in India, with clear boundaries between them. The word for "conversion" in several Indian languages is literally "change of religion". It is not talking about inner spiritual change, but a change of religious community.

3. "It's too easy"

Some Hindus will object to the idea of free forgiveness. It runs contrary to the teaching of *karma*: everyone must face the consequences of their actions and find their own path. The desire to work things out for oneself is very deep. But this is not cheap grace. Christ's followers are called to the highest standards as they respond to God's love. Jesus' Sermon on the Mount shows this. But this new way of life is only possible because Jesus has died in our place and taken the consequences of our wrongdoing and shame, which we could never do.

4. "We have many stories: you have only one"

Hindus glory in the breadth of the many beliefs, stories and philosophies in their tradition. By contrast the Christian story can seem so narrow, as Pi thought when he first heard about the cross:

> What a downright weird story ... I asked for another story, one that I might find more satisfying ... But Father Martin made me understand that the stories that came before it ... were simply prologue to the Christians. Their religion had one Story, and to it they came back again and again, over and over.

This seemed a grave limitation. But as Pi reflected on the story:

> I couldn't get Him out of my head... and the more I learned about Him, the less I wanted to leave Him.
> *Life of Pi*

We keep coming back to the same story.

But it is important to show how the "other" stories throughout the Bible fit into the "big story" and point to Jesus. For example, the creation and fall, God's covenant with his people, their failure to keep God's law, the sacrifices, and the prophecies of the Old Testament. They all fit together.

Social and cultural concerns

Hindu objections may be theological, such as the challenge to the uniqueness of Jesus. But just as important may be social and cultural concerns. If you are born into your community of faith, then the thought of leaving it is hard, if not impossible. We have already seen the strength of family ties. Are they being asked to "leave your community and join ours"? Would that be a betrayal of their family? Some fear losing face in the community, or repercussions if they break caste rules.

Following Jesus does not necessarily imply a change of community or culture. At the same time, it does bring a person into a relationship with other followers of Christ. It means being part of a wider group and in some sense identifying with them. There will be changes; loyalty to Christ has a cost. We shall look at this further in the next chapter and also consider the challenges this raises for the church.

Spiritual barriers

While there is only one God, people have different ideas about God—what Hindus call different forms or manifestations. Some of these may agree with the character of God revealed in the Bible. Others do not. There are different spiritual powers to which people have allegiance. These are often expressed in necklaces, amulets and bracelets, marked with the image of their chosen deity or guru and blessed in a ceremony to give special protection. Gurus can exercise strong control. Some people have fear of their deities, or of malevolent spirits. Others face habits and temptations which they are not able to overcome. They may have deep personal needs.

These issues face people of all faith backgrounds and none. The Bible is clear that we are all under the power of forces that keep us from God. That is why prayer and belief in God's grace are a central part of our engagement.

Reflect

- Look again at the questions in this chapter. Which of them have you met in your conversations with your Hindu friends?
- Are there other questions that you have encountered?
- Think through the answers that you would give.
- Read again the comments on the question "Why did Jesus say he was the only way?" (pages 97-100). Do they make sense to you? Discuss them with a Christian friend, so that the ideas are clear in your mind.
- Take time to pray again for your friends, thinking particularly of these and other questions they may have.

Chapter twelve

How should a church engage with Hindus?

Christ's followers are not simply individuals. Just as family and community are important foundations of Hindu identity, so Christ's followers are linked to each other, part of a close-knit group that we call the church. This has implications in both directions.

The word "church" may suggest buildings and institutions, pronouncements by church officials, sometimes scandals. Hindus often identify it with their understanding of cultural Christianity, as well as what is projected by the media. There is a history—not always good—and particularly in India there are legal and social boundaries between religious communities, as we have noted. "New Agers"—Westerners who have adopted Hindu thought and religious practices—may have preconceptions from their previous experience of Christianity.

But the church is actually people—the followers of Christ. It could be a regular church congregation, or a group of students or some other informal grouping. They could meet anywhere. How do Hindus and this local group of people, whether very large or just a few people, relate to each other?

The challenge

This local group of Christ's followers should be a welcoming, loving community of warm relationships, worshipping and learning together, and engaging with the community around them—including Hindus, of course—as they love and serve them and celebrate the good news of Jesus. But how do we inspire our church to be like that? Many of us have a long way to go.

How do we also learn to cross cultural boundaries, so that people of different cultural backgrounds will feel at home and be able to "hear" what we are trying to say? In today's world most of the people outside the church will struggle to understand or feel comfortable with the language and culture of our churches—including Hindus.

These are big challenges! We need first to be committed to reach out cross-culturally, which will be both intentional and sacrificial. Then we need to shape our worship, teaching, community life and outreach so that they communicate the good news in ways that are understood in different cultures. We also need to create space where our Hindu friends will feel welcome when we invite them.

Here are some ways that a local church can do this.

1. Inclusion and belonging

It is important for a church to reach out to include Hindus. We have already spoken about doing things together, finding common concerns and looking for joint activities (see pages 69-71). This breaks down barriers and builds relationships of trust. Remember that some Hindus view "the church" with suspicion. The great majority do not, but may still have misunderstandings and are quite content with their own community. The church needs to be a community that genuinely "loves its neighbour as itself".

For example, in London, one church runs a charity shop as part of its service to the community. Several of the volunteers are Hindus. Working together, they have developed relationships of friendship and trust. Another church ran quarterly "Bollywood evenings" with food, film, music and entertainment, which were very popular in the community.

This gives a sense of belonging, being part of a group that genuinely welcomes all.

2. Experiencing spiritual reality

As the church includes people in this way, it will be natural to welcome them to take part in the church's spiritual activities, whether that is a regular Sunday meeting or a more informal group for discussion and prayer.

Some churches organise booktables in the local market, to give out literature, talk to people and pray with them. Some offer prayer for healing or personal needs. Others organise special events at Christmas or Easter (or perhaps around *Diwali*) or any special occasion, with food (vegetarian, of course!), music and a special speaker.

These activities enable people to experience spiritual reality, whether that is values of love and welcome, service and equal treatment of all, or prayer, joyful devotion, praise to Jesus and hearing God speak. For Hindus experiencing this kind of group, it may be what first attracts them to Jesus or challenges their perception that all paths are the same. This kind of group is a demonstration of the good news.

A church needs to ask what kind of spiritual experience visitors will encounter, from the initial welcome (warm? friendly?) onwards. Would they feel that this is a group that shows true devotion to Christ? Would they sense his presence and peace? What changes will your church need to make?

Timothy Paul, who works with the Gujarati Hindu community in the USA, has developed an approach to outreach called MARG: Making Authentic Relationships Grow. It is a pathway of spiritual discovery and gradual acceptance and surrender to the reality of Jesus as the Lord, who brings salvation within Hindu culture. There are five steps on this journey:

1. **Relationship (*Sabandh*)**: building authentic, respectful relationships.
2. **Experience (*Anubhav*)**: experiencing spiritual reality, especially the reality and power of prayer.
3. **Devotion (*Bhakti*)**: joining in worship to Jesus through thanksgiving, singing and prayer.
4. **Sacrifice (*Balidan*)**: learning about the central truth of Jesus' sacrificial death and resurrection.

5. **Surrender (*Sharanam*)**: inviting people to surrender to Jesus—without calling them to give up their Hindu cultural heritage.

He says that in this process "it seems that Hindus grow to love Jesus before they come to know him in an exclusive relationship", but in the end he becomes for them "*Muktinath*, the lord of salvation".

We spoke earlier about creating space. That means intentionally creating an environment where it is safe for Hindu friends to explore, to ask and to be in process in understanding the gospel, rather than an environment where they are pressured to make a decision to "become a Christian".

Will they encounter people at your church who (wrongly) assume that they are already Christian or are actively considering conversion to Christianity? Or will they encounter people who are interested to ask questions and understand them—and not pounce on them?

In other words, is your church community as a whole actively expecting visitors to be present, so that when someone comes, people do not say awkward or off-putting things to them? Preachers can do the same thing by assuming that everyone present is a believer, and by denouncing others in an unhelpful way. We need to cultivate a culture in our churches where people who are searching and questioning do not feel condemned and judged as they do so, but are loved and encouraged as we wait patiently to see signs of the Spirit's work in them.

A church can also ask what kind of cultural experience visitors would have. Would they understand the language or appreciate the music? Does the food include vegetarian choices? (For many Hindus vegetarianism is a major cultural and spiritual issue.) Are the leaders and the style of activity all from one culture? Would visitors to your church feel like this woman?

> My experiences of trying to fit in with other Christian communities have been very difficult—from differences in food and humour to being left out in conversations because I was the only Indian in the group.

A church may make cultural mistakes, but those can be overlooked where there is genuine love and the lives of members demonstrate their message. Friendship, integrity and hospitality remain the essentials.

> I still remember the awkwardness of my first visit to church—the looking back, nervous, worried about what my friends and family would say. Would they disown me? Was I betraying my community and culture, by going to what we saw as a Western institution—because for many of us, Jesus Christ was the white man's God. I even pictured him as a city gent, complete with pin-striped suit and bowler hat!
>
> My first instinct when I entered the church building was to remove my shoes, as I had always done before entering a holy place— but everybody else was keeping their shoes on. Then I saw a carpeted area—perfect for sitting on to worship God. I headed towards it, but was directed to wooden pews which

were most uncomfortable. And then to top it all, the organ started playing—and I thought, "My goodness, who's died?" because I associated the organ with funerals. I struggled through the service until the sermon was preached—I was hooked. I came back week after week, just to hear the sermon while suffering through the other bits, but I would make sure to leave without talking to anybody.

Several weeks later, the minister invited newcomers to a meal at his home. This was the turning point for me as it gave me an opportunity to get to know some of the leaders and fellow students. The church was no longer a sea of unknown faces.

Ram Gidoomal

3. Finding the right group

For many churches, providing this kind of spiritual experience and making people feel at home in the larger group of the congregation is too big a challenge. It is often helpful—and in many cases essential—for someone exploring the Christian faith to be part of a smaller group in which they can relate to others from similar backgrounds. This is a place to feel more at home culturally, to ask questions from those who have gone through similar experiences and to develop relationships.

It was several years after I became a Christian that I attended a group in which somebody prayed in Gujarati. I was amazed—until then I thought that God only understood English.   *Jai*

> I embraced Christ within a Baptist church, but for a time I also attended an Asian support group, which was invaluable in helping me grasp that I could affirm my Indian identity and be a Christian. At the support group we understood each other's struggles. *Ramesh*

If your church is not able to provide such a group, you may need to look for other churches or groups that can help.

Many Hindus take part in a *satsang* (literally "truth gathering" or "together to the truth"), a regular or occasional group meeting in a hall or a home for singing and prayer. Some churches have organised *Isu satsangs* (*Isu* = Jesus in Gujarati). This kind of group can be geared very specifically to a particular culture, if that is appropriate.

Those in a small group like this need to feel welcome also in the larger group where people of all cultural backgrounds are loved and affirmed.

4. The importance of family and community.

Ask friends and visitors to your church about their family and look for ways to reach out and welcome the whole family rather than just the individual.

As your church welcomes people and invites them to experience the reality of your devotion to Christ, some will show interest or want to follow Jesus as well. But don't expect them to change their culture, eat different food, or dress differently. These things are not part of the gospel that gives us peace with God, and they count as "additions" to the gospel. But sometimes the pressure to conform can be very subtle.

To counterbalance this tendency, take an active interest in people's cultural background and look for proactive ways to affirm it. That could range from food and music to different ways of praying or meditation. Our concern is not for people to "change their community" but for all of us to follow Christ while remaining within our culture and our communities, as far as we can.

It is important to communicate this truth, especially to young people, so that they do not feel they have to make a break with their family, or speak rashly to their parents. They need first to experience and demonstrate change in their lives.

We can also exert pressure on people to attend a lot of meetings, as though this is the way to show devotion. It is important to give time and space for people to stay within their family. Here is one man's experience:

> When I began to follow Christ it was like a huge bomb being set off in my family. My mother said that the family were being punished because my father had failed to perform certain prayers for his dead parents. Blaming him didn't go down too well, as you can imagine! They feared that it would have a detrimental affect on my sister's marriage prospects. They were also concerned for my welfare because they were aware of Christian cults. There was plenty of emotional blackmail, as I was repeatedly told that I would drive them to a premature death.
>
> By failing to spend time then with my family and their friends, I lost the opportunity to dem-

onstrate what it means to be a follower of Christ. Now as I try to rebuild some of those bridges people are suspicious of my motives.

The situation may arise where a person's family shows great displeasure if they express commitment to Christ. In that case the church family needs to be there for them, showing love and support without undermining their own family.

First-generation followers of Christ often find themselves caught between their family, which neither understands nor accepts their decision, and the church, which does not always seem to understand either.

They want to communicate the good news of Jesus with family and friends, with whom they have been so closely bound together, but who may now misunderstand them and are also suffering because of their actions. There may be a real cost for the new believers and their family that can last for years. The church must understand this and support them.

5. Understand that this is a process

Hindus are used to absorbing new ideas and spiritual paths. So to show interest in Christ, or begin to follow him, is not necessarily a big step. Many are very happy to adapt and incorporate Christian ideas and concepts into their existing framework.

I was in a Bible study and one student started talking about how important it is that we consider our eternal destiny .... in my follow-up discussion with him I discovered he was talking about the importance of remembering to create good karma.

To work through all the implications of commitment to Christ, and Christ alone, is a process that can be lengthy. Each person will respond to God's truth in different ways and the Holy Spirit must guide them. Here is a typical example:

> First I put a picture of Jesus along with the other gods on the shelf where I worshipped. After a time he became the main focus of my prayers, as he was the one who answered my prayers. Eventually he became the only God whom I worship.

So don't push or be in a hurry. Don't argue or criticise. Go on showing friendship and love. Give time; open your home and family as far as this is possible. And go on praying.

Much more could be written about the questions and challenges for a Hindu working out a new commitment, or for those guiding them. Many of these are discussed in greater detail in *Notes for the Journey: Following Jesus, Staying South Asian.*

There are also helpful personal accounts and discussions of issues in *Walking the Way of the Cross with our Hindu Friends.* See the resource list, p 121.

Summary

Here are seven steps that your church—or perhaps a smaller group withing the church—could take:

1. **Gather a group that starts praying together** for Hindu friends.

2. **Think together about local "justice" or "mercy" projects** and ways to involve local Hindu friends in this with you. See the suggestions earlier on pages 66-68.

3. **Think about ways to include Hindus in existing activities,** such as mother and toddler groups, homework clubs or other youth activities, keep fit, etc. It's vital that church members also develop genuine friendships with them outside these activities.

4. **Arrange training for your church members** to welcome Hindu (and other) visitors with culturally understandable love and friendship, while still giving them space.

5. **Take a group from your church to visit a local Hindu temple** to learn more about what Hindus believe. Then meet later to discuss and pray.

6. **Host a special event** (Easter, Christmas, a Bollywood evening, a business speaker; serving Indian food; perhaps with Indian music).

7. **Consider forming a smaller group for study, prayer, singing and worship** that can relate more specifically to Hindus. Resources are available to help develop groups like this (see resources, p 121).

Bible passages

1. Our approach to people of any faith

Acts 17 v 22-31

Look carefully at Paul's approach to people with their own religion (which was very similar to some branches of Hinduism):

- Paul acknowledges and speaks respectfully to them about their religious devotion (v 22-23), despite his inner feelings (v 16).
- Paul knows about their beliefs and connects with what they have in common:
  - the Creator God (v 24-26a)
  - the universal sense of God (v 27b-28)
  - that we can know God and can search for him (v 26b-27a).
- Paul corrects their view of images of God (v 24b, 25, 29).
- Paul shows that the coming of Jesus brings decisive change and calls for repentance (v 30-31).

Acts 10 v 1-8, 34-43

- *What did Peter learn about God's approach to people who seek him, from any background? (See v 34-35 and also v 1-4.)*
- *Who did Peter focus on in his message to Cornelius and what did he call for?*

1 Corinthians 9 v 19-23

- *Make a list of all the practical lessons Paul gives us for reaching people of different cultures for Christ.*

Luke 18 v 9-14
- *What is God looking for?*
- *Why is this a surprise for religious people of any background, including those with a Christian background?*

2. Passages about Jesus to share with your Hindu friends

Summaries of Jesus' life and ministry
- Matthew 4 v 23-25; Acts 2 v 22-24; 10 v 36-43

People Jesus mixed with
- Matthew 8 v 1-11; John 8 v 1-11; 3 v 1-2; Luke 7 v 36-38; 14 v 1; Mark 2 v 15

Jesus' lifestyle
- Luke 9 v 57-58; John 11 v 35-36; 8 v 46; Mark 14 v 55

Jesus' invitation and claims
- Matthew 11 v 28; John 8 v 31-32; Mark 2 v 5-11; Matthew 7 v 28-29; John 10 v 30-33

Why did Jesus come?

- John 10 v 10-11; Mark 10 v 45; Luke 19 v 10

Why did Jesus die?

- 1 Peter 2 v 24; 2 Corinthians 5 v 21; Luke 24 v 25-26, 45-48; Isaiah 53 v 5-9 (prophecy of his death, hundreds of years before)
- Each of the Gospels describes Jesus' death and resurrection in detail. It may be appropriate to read the whole of Matthew 26 – 28; Mark 14 – 16; Luke 22 – 24 or John 18 – 21 with your friends.

Who is Jesus?

- **Jesus shows us God:** John 1 v 18; 10 v 30; 14 v 9-10
- **Jesus gives eternal life:** John 3 v 16; 6 v 35; 11 v 25
- **Jesus is the treasure and priceless pearl:** Matthew 13 v 44-46; Colossians 1 v 27; 2 v 3

Resources

Books

- Burnett, David *Spirit of Hinduism*, Monarch, 2006
- Gandhi, M., *An autobiography: the story of my experiments with Truth*, Navijivan, 1927
- Gidoomal, Ram, *Sari'n' chips*, Kingsway/SAC, 1993
- Knott, Kim, *A very short introduction to Hinduism*, Oxford University Press, 1998
- Richard, H.L., *Hinduism*, William Carey Library, Pasadena, 1998, 2001
- Scott, Basil, *God Has No Favourites: The New Testament on First Century Religions*, Primalogue, 2013
- Thomson, Robin, *Changing India: insights from the margin*, BRPC, 2002 (distributed in the UK by South Asian Concern)
- Viswanathan, Ed, *Am I a Hindu?* The Hinduism Primer, Rupa and Co, Calcutta, 1993

More detailed studies

- Basham A. L., *The Sacred Cow: The Evolution of Classical Hinduism*, edited by Kenneth G Zysk, Rider, 1989
- Brockington, John, *Hinduism and Christianity*, Macmillan, London, 1992
- Fuller, C. J., *The Camphor Flame: Popular Hinduism and Society in India*, Princeton University Press, 1992
- Hopkins, T. J., *The Hindu Religious Tradition: The Religious Life of Man*, Wadsworth Publishing Co, California, 1971
- Kanitkar, V. P., and Cole, Owen, *Hinduism*: Teach Yourself Books, World Faiths, Hodder, 1995
- Mangalwadi, Vishal *The world of Gurus* Cornerstone Press, Chicago, 1992

Christian approaches

- Acharya Daya Prakash *Fulfilment of the Vedic Pilgrimage in the Lord Jesus Christ*, 2nd edtion, OM Books, 2004
- Alexander, Ellen and Thomson, Robin, (eds), *Walking the Way of the Cross with our Hindu Friends*, Interserve, Bangalore, 2011. With accompanying DVD.
- Bharati, Dayanand, *Living Water and Indian Bowl*, 1997, 2012

- Davda, Sonal, Shivdasani, Suneel, Thomson, Robin and Wardell, Margaret, *Looking for Directions: towards an Asian spirituality*, South Asian Concern, 2006
- Gamadia, Dr Sam, *Christian Approach to Hinduism*
- Gidoomal, Ram and Wardell, Margaret, *Chapatis for Tea*, Highland, 1994
- Guptara, Prabhu and Osmaston, Amiel, *Yoga—A Christian Option?* Grove Books Ltd, 1987
- Maharaj, Rabi, *Death of a Guru*, Hodder, 1978
- Mahtani, Deepak and Celia, Sindhi *Journeys of Faith*, 2010
- *Masala Discovery Groups*, South Asian Concern
- Rasiah, C. and Thomson, Robin, *Notes for the Journey: Following Jesus, Staying South Asian*, South Asian Concern, 2011
- Richard, H.L., *Following Jesus in the Hindu Context*: N. V. Tilak, William Carey Library, Pasadena, 1998, 2001
- Sutcliffe, Sally (ed), *Good News for Asians in Britain*, Grove Books Ltd, 1998

Video/DVD
- Coming to Britain: *An Immigrant's story*, CTA, distributed by Trinity Vision
- *Daya Sagar*

Websites
- www.southasianconcern.org
- www.karma2grace.com
- www.aradhnamusic.com/ (Indian-style worship music)

Evangelistic
- *Jesus through Asian Eyes: 16 Frequently asked Questions*, Good Book Company, 2014 (with study course)
  UK: www.thegoodbook.co.uk
  USA: www.thegoodbook.com
- *Christianity Explored*, The Good Book Company, 2012. For those with English as a second language, there is also a *Universal Edition* of *Christianity Explored* that uses clear and simple English.

Organisations

Australia
Culture Connect, a ministry of Interserve Australia
www.cultureconnect.net.au

UK
South Asian Concern
info@southasianconcern.org
www.southasianconcern.org

South Asian Forum of the Evangelical Alliance
saf@eauk.org
www.eauk.org/saf

USA
11 days of prayer posts information for prayer and other resources for ministry among Hindus. It is linked to the Rethinking Forum (rethinkingforum.com):
www. 11daysofprayer.org

Christar is an evangelical mission working worldwide among Buddhists, Hindus, Muslims and others.
www.christar.org/go/locations/north-america

Go Network provides resources to help in reproducing spiritually healthy networks of God's Kingdom within Hindu communities worldwide
www.gonetworkonline.com

International Journal of Frontier Missiology has a good selection of articles from the archives and current issues
www.ijfm.org

International Students Inc
An evangelical group working with international students (the parent body of what is now Friends International in the UK)
www.isionline.org is the website for Christians
www.internationalstudents.org is the website for students

IVCF's International Student Ministry (ISM)
ism.intervarsity.org

Messengers of God's Love Multilingual
Literature and other resources in many languages
www.multilingual-southasian.com

www.nayajeevan.org is a website for welcoming South Asians to their new life in North America.

South Asian Friendship Center, Chicago
A drop in centre in Chicago's "Little India" including daily ministry to Hindus
www.safcchicago.com
see the section 'What we offer'

YWAM's Contextual Ministry
among Hindus
www.hindustudy.com/

Please note: The websites and organisations listed above are, to the best of our knowledge, reliable and trustworthy at the time of going to press. Visit the webpage for this book for an up to date list of organisations and contacts: Get in touch with us if you would like to list your organisation in this resource.
www.thegoodbook.co.uk

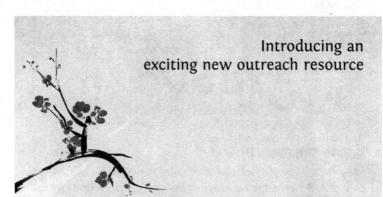

Discovering

Jesus

through Asian eyes

thegoodbook
COMPANY

Discovering

Jesus

through Asian eyes

What's the opportunity?

Millions of people with an Asian background live in the West. Some have only recently arrived, others have lived in the West for many generations. Asians are often more open to talking about spiritual things than many longer-established residents.

How can one resource speak to such a diverse group of people?

It might seem strange to create a set of resources that tries to speak to people with such a diverse range of beliefs and cultures. What could be more different than Buddhism and Islam? What do Japanese people and Bangladeshis have in common?

But Asians of all kinds share many attitudes in common: an openness to talking about spiritual things; a feeling that they must live up to family expectations; a sense of honour. But most of all, they share the view that Christianity is a western religion.

The outreach booklet and course pick up on these common cultural ways of thinking to present the good news about Jesus in a way that is open, friendly and appealing.

What is the *Jesus through Asian eyes* booklet?

This full-colour booklet is designed to be given to Asians of any background. It asks and answers 16 of the most frequently asked questions that people have about Jesus, Christianity and faith in God. It is filled with warm testimonies from Asian people from all kinds of backgrounds who have discovered the love of God in Christ.

The questions are answered carefully from the Bible in a way that is culturally sensitive and gently leads the reader towards belief in Jesus. The booklet is designed to be given to anyone from an Asian background – a neighbour, friend or colleague from work.

How does the course work?

The *Discovering Jesus through Asian eyes* course is based on the booklet. If someone has read the booklet and wants to know more, you can invite them to join you to explore the questions in a little more depth. The course is split into eight sessions which each look at two questions from the booklet. The emphasis is on friendly, open discussions, which look at passages from the Bible. The studies have been extensively trialled and tested with a wide variety of Asian people.

What materials are available?

- The *Jesus through Asian eyes* booklet is a beautifully designed and produced 32-page colourful booklet. You can buy it for as little as £1 per copy when you purchase in bulk.

- The *Leader's Guide* contains everything you need to know to run a course – extensive notes on the discussion questions, helpful advice on how to address issues unique to different people groups and religions, and ideas for promoting the course, and conducting outreach to Asians in your local area.

- The *Discussion Guide* is for each person who attends a course. It contains questions, Bible passages, plus testimonies and explanations of difficult terms.

- Dedicated website at **www.discovering-jesus.com**

- Promotional flyers and posters available, plus training events.

Leader's Guide

Booklet

Discussion Guide

thegoodbook
COMPANY

Opening up the Bible

At The Good Book Company, we are dedicated to helping Christians and local churches grow. We believe that God's growth process always starts with hearing clearly what he has said to us through his timeless word—the Bible.

Ever since we opened our doors in 1991, we have been striving to produce resources that honour God in the way the Bible is used. We have grown to become an international provider of user-friendly resources to the Christian community, with believers of all backgrounds and denominations using our Bible studies, books, evangelistic resources, DVD-based courses and training events.

We want to equip ordinary Christians to live for Christ day by day, and churches to grow in their knowledge of God, their love for one another, and the effectiveness of their outreach.

Call us for a discussion of your needs or visit one of our local websites for more information on the resources and services we provide.

UK & Europe: www.thegoodbook.co.uk
North America: www.thegoodbook.com
Australia: www.thegoodbook.com.au
New Zealand: www.thegoodbook.co.nz

UK & Europe: 0333 123 0880
North America: 866 244 2165
Australia: (02) 6100 4211
New Zealand (+64) 3 343 1990

www.christianityexplored.org

Our partner site is a great place for those exploring the Christian faith, with a clear explanation of the good news, powerful testimonies and answers to difficult questions.

One life! What's it all about?